MOVEMENT EDUCATION
The Place of Movement in Physical Education

MEGAN M. BRIGGS

Senior Dance Teacher to Halifax Education Authority

MACDONALD & EVANS LTD.

8 JOHN STREET, LONDON WCIN 2HY

1974

First published July 1974

©

MACDONALD AND EVANS LIMITED
1974

ISNB: 0 7121 1379 7

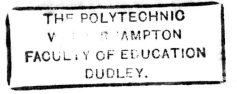
Printed in Great Britain by

J. W. ARROWSMITH LIMITED
BRISTOL BS3 2NT

FOREWORD

Successful movement training for teachers is the first essential in successful movement education for children. All students should be movement specialists and qualified in all branches of physical education where movement appertains. Why should children be limited in school to a programme of physical education, which is designed for the particular bent and talent of the teacher rather than for the needs of the children? How many dance specialists—those who have had studio training—are there in contact with children in schools?

The following four-year course, preferably achieving graduate status, is offered as a suggestion.

1. A two-year general physical education course concerned with the theory and practice of:

(*a*) basic movement and its development into educational gymnastics and educational dance closely allied to movement observation and movement memory training—in other words, movement education;
(*b*) educational gymnastics;
(*c*) educational dance;
(*d*) games—traditional and creative;
(*e*) athletics;
(*f*) swimming;
(*g*) recreational pursuits, *e.g.* riding, fencing, skating, etc.

2. A third year with special emphasis on educational dance to be spent at the Art of Movement Studio, Addlestone, Surrey.

3. A fourth year with special emphasis on educational gymnastics.

Throughout the course the work should at all times be closely related to the teaching, coaching and observation of children. In addition the course should include a study of the relationship of creative moment education to other arts subjects, the care and maintenance of equipment, and organisation of practical problems in physical education, for example, showers, physical education uniform, etc. A great many students enter the teaching profession with very little or scant knowledge of such matters; some, when confronted with the organisation of their first sports day, are at a complete loss. The Education course, which is compulsory in all teacher training, should, in the author's opinion, be integrated with and allied to the work in physical education, and should not be regarded as a separate course where the link with the specialist subject is left to the imagination of the student. Teaching practice should consist of working with all age groups and with children of different aptitudes and abilities, not merely the training for and teaching of one particular age-group. As most large schools employ a nurse or welfare officer, remedial gymnastics, first aid, anatomy and physiology are no longer necessarily an essential part of physical-education training, but could be included if desired. To fail an anatomy and physiology examination should not, however, debar a student from entering the teaching profession, as has been the case in the past, regardless of how good or capable a teacher of physical education they may be.

M.M.B.

PREFACE

This book is intended for the physical education specialist (student and teacher) and also the non-specialist teacher who, in primary and often in secondary schools, has to undertake the movement education of both boys and girls. In addition, it is also intended to help those trained by formal methods who now have to cope with rethinking and retraining within the field of Movement. To this end it has been written in basic language which can be understood by all those mentioned above, and a glossary of terms has been included.

Many books have been written on a specific branch of physical education and for a specific age-group. This book defines Movement and its place in the physical education programme, relates how it fulfils its task *per se* and in the various branches of that programme, and indicates its place in the educational life of a school. The border-line between gymnastics and dance is also defined to eliminate an all too prevalent confusion which still exists today. In support of theoretical ideas a skeletal syllabus is set out to illustrate what could otherwise be regarded by some as physical education platitudes. The book's practical purpose is to give concise guidance in the presentation, subsequent development and progression of movement education for children.

A great amount of the material content is the creative work and ideas of children of different ages and abilities. I have included this to demonstrate what children are capable of producing when using a movement vocabulary as a means to an end. That end is purposeful, creative and expressive work in all branches of physical education, with a high standard of performance particularly in gymnastics and dance. My intention is to provide an example of how to meet the children's needs and to guide them in developing and perfecting their own ideas, which is the ultimate aim of all modern educational methods.

The chapters on modern educational gymnastics are particularly important for the actual apparatus content. Many children today, though working by modern methods, still use the apparatus designed for formal work. I have attempted to show in these chapters how children can utilise this apparatus to suit their creative needs in planning their own apparatus framework, tasks and sequences. The plan for a movement gymnasium, in allowing for combination and continuity of floor and apparatus work, offers a solution to one of the most pressing problems arising in gymnastics—how to transfer good floor work on to apparatus without losing quality of movement.

Finally I would like to acknowledge the work of the pupils of the Percy Jackson Grammar School, Woodlands, near Doncaster, and my debt to the teachings of Rudolf Laban which have been freely drawn upon in the text; and also to express my thanks to Mr. D. K. H. Briggs for the photographic illustrations.

M.M.B.

March 1974

CONTENTS

Chapter One

INTRODUCTION

THE TASK OF MODERN PHYSICAL EDUCATION

It is still the opinion of many experts in this field that the task of modern physical education is to set sufficient challenge and scope for the ability of the gifted child, and at the same time to ensure that the average or less gifted, and less willing, child is extended to its fullest capabilities and that scope is given for improvement and achievement by all.

Having given the child freedom of expression and licence to create, we must ensure that it understands what to do with this freedom and how to use it to its best purpose. Our task is to enable the child to channel its ability and freedom of expression in the right direction. This has a bearing upon the whole pattern and structure of education, as one of the major problems today in the school society is the inability of the child to take responsibility for its own actions and hence the actions of others in the community. It is to an increasingly large number no longer a privilege to bear responsibility for the school and "house" as an active and useful way of contributing to school life. Instead, this is looked upon as an unwelcome chore and burden lacking in benefits or payment of some sort in order to make it worthwhile.

Children are constantly grumbling that " 'prefects' are not given authority," without realising that authority cannot be handed over as a commodity. It is achieved, in fact, by the impression of one's personality upon the mass or individual. In the present educational system teachers themselves must face a similar problem. It is, however, a fact that some "support-demanding" young people will enter training colleges, and later schools, presumably nurturing the same complaint as to the basis of their authority.

It is the author's belief, however, that today it is not the system or process of education which makes the teacher—as in the past, when to be sent to the Head was for a child the ultimate and final punishment—but rather the reverse, where the teacher is responsible for the system or process of education himself and must, on matters of subject and personal contact with children, be self-supporting and self-reliant.

It is yet again the opinion of many experts in the field of physical education that we must, in this subject, attempt to go further than the development of or concentration on the practice and attainment of physical skills. This aim is still vitally necessary, but we have to consider hand in hand with this the use of physical education as an aid to the creative and aesthetic development of the child, and how and where in the different branches of physical education the possibilities for doing this occur.

Educational dance should provide opportunities for the following:

1. The development of basic movement into dance.
2. Creative dance composition.
3. Dramatic movement, dance mime and dance drama.
4. Percussion and dance accompaniment.

For the teacher, a study of the contribution of this work to the education and development of the child, which is not to be assessed in only physical terms, is essential. Furthermore, this work can be effective only when it is related to the observation, teaching and coaching of children at all levels.

Dance is the blending of freedom and discipline: it develops the child's ability and willingness to follow guidance as well as satisfying its need for free invention and use of the imagination. The task of the teacher is to use movement and dance as an educational medium. This can be done only when the work in this field is based on the teacher's movement observation and hence her subsequent assessment of the needs of a particular class.

Educational gymnastics should provide opportunities for the following:

1. The mastery of movement—of body movement and body agility—on the floor.

2. The development of physical skills with regard to apparatus, the mastery of movement on the same, and the ability to think out (or to carry out) creative ideas and hence to perform creative movement on apparatus.

3. The development of the child's ability to meet the challenge that apparatus work offers.

THE PROBLEMS OF PHYSICAL EDUCATION

The examination of the task of physical education leads us to consider the problems which arise when carrying out this task. One of the major issues is the question as to whether or not this modern method has trained children to think as well as to perform. The old or formal way was to imitate an action and follow direct instructions. Direct teaching concerned itself chiefly with the training of the body with application of thought, whilst indirect teaching now concerns itself with the fusion of body, mind and personality. Children, however, who are lazy thinkers or who react slowly to teaching stimulus present a greater problem than they did previously when the main responsibility for and the drive of the lesson came from the teacher; now the initiative rests still on the teacher but also with the children, thus enabling them to take a greater part in and to contribute more to the lesson. Great care, however, must be taken today to see that all children in the class do work and do not merely act as passengers.

Without doubt, the children who are gifted gain far more with this modern approach as the boundaries to which they can go are less limited than before and they have endless possibilities to explore. For the less able but extremely hard-working children the modern method is ideally suited to their needs. They now have an opportunity at least to take an active and creative part in the lesson and have the chance of achievement that before was not possible, unless they could perform the specific and often only task set by relying upon others or upon the gymnast to hoist them over apparatus.

It is a significant factor that in the old way much of the work had to be "recapped" or repeated from lesson to lesson, while from the modern method it would appear that what children discover and find out for themselves, or are guided to discover, they remember and retain more easily.

As physical educationalists we now have the task of educating the mind, the body and the emotions—a task which requires that the children possess freedom of expression, but also an underlying iron discipline. It is preferable that this discipline is self-discipline, for children must learn how to use freedom in order to justify their possession of it. The emotions and feelings of the present generation at school have erupted into dance and music, and we are faced with the task of educating these emotions. This is a significant factor in education, for previously children tended to live by their logic and reasoning and controlled their emotions—the accent was on suppression rather than expression. Today's youth live by their feelings and emotions, are swayed considerably by them and hence are much more vulnerable. The manner in which children themselves cope with the problem of adjustment is a factor which cannot be ignored and the importance of dance as an educational and remedial factor must be recognised.

In order to help children cope with the problem of self-discipline perhaps in the more formative and initial stages of child development we need a little more discipline imposed on children or a firmer contact with them. It is possible to be kind but firm and by this method the child can acquire a self-taught discipline or a realisation of discipline. Our task is also to enable children to think about behaviour as well as about movement patterns.

Education has changed certainly, but have the fundamental needs of children and the children themselves changed? They have changed physiologically and sociologically, but what about their fundamental needs? If the latter have (or have not) changed, is the present system of education suited to these needs? Teachers, especially those with a long period of teaching experience, can best honestly answer this question. In the author's opinion it must be answered in terms of assessing character, personality, loyalty, and responsibility—qualities which the young today often tend to ignore or of which they have no cognisance. Education is, after all, not concerned solely with the gaining of university places, nor with filling the world with academic "zombies" or educated "louts."

Having examined and dealt with problems concerned with the educational aspect, certain problems arise with specific bearing upon the subject of physical education. Consideration must be given as to whether or not we need to set tasks for the children. This depends upon the needs of the class but it should be pointed out that there is a strong case for setting *movement* tasks on the floor which can then be applied to apparatus in the gymnasium. On the apparatus children must still be made aware of the effort actions of pushing, pulling and swinging, etc., or a combination of these. They also need to be made aware of the amount of impetus, impact or run required, otherwise they will slither and flop in their work, for children do not naturally or accidentally stumble across the most economic and "effortful" way of using apparatus. To achieve this aim one can choose between several possible approaches to the class:

1. Suggest to the class.
2. Question the class.
3. Stimulate thought process.
4. Allow the class to experiment.
5. Encourage the class to offer their solutions to a problem.
6. Consider alternatives, *e.g.* "which?" or "in what way?"
7. Allow the children by demonstration to illustrate their ideas and solutions to a problem.

In the first flush of creative physical education the important factor was that a child worked at its own rate, within its own capabilities or limitations. Did we attempt to improve the rate sufficiently and to extend the child's capabilities and limitations? We still look for the skilled performer and for the mastery of movement and the meeting of challenges in a skilful way as well as the inner attitude and expressive and dramatic qualities in dance. Let us, however, examine this question of whether or not to set with reference to the task of movement.

The first consideration must be one of approach: can movement training cope with increasing physical maturity and, in spite of this, ensure control of body weight, or should it work with regard to and with acceptance of the limitations of children with excess weight? Secondly, can it cope with the needs of children of different age, ability and aptitude? Thirdly, there is the question of different sizes of children's bodies and their individual needs although they are all in one corporate form or class.

The ideal solution to the problem is, it is said, to strike a balance between the children's individual, emotional and physical needs. This is indeed a worthwhile end-product, but in order to achieve it we must strike a balance between the application of Rudolf Laban's principles and the underlying principles of physical education. Also, some of the principles of formal work must be applied to modern methods in order to obtain, for example, the effort actions so essential in the gymnasium. We can say "Push" to a child but unless that child understands what "Push" is and what makes "Push" he cannot do it. We are still making children aware of these fundamental principles even if the method of so doing has changed. If we did not we would get slithering, sliding and unco-ordinated bodies. In the author's opinion the answer lies in making children aware personally, not in merely telling them or asking them to imitate a demonstration.

Children can get an enormous sense of achievement from meeting the challenge of physical education entirely by themselves, in their own way, but some classes need to be given the opportunity to meet the teacher's challenge, her teaching challenge—the teacher still being the focal point of the class.

There are a variety of teaching methods that can be used, and it is experience of movement and teaching children which is the best guide as to which method to choose according to the individual needs of a particular class. The various methods are as follows:

1. For the class to experiment and then for the teacher to teach.
2. For the teacher to teach and then for the class to experiment.
3. For the class to experiment and then for the teacher to guide the class.
4. For the class to experiment only.

When we consider the material as well as the method the variety increases—there would appear to be a distinct division between old and new methods, and a state where the two meet sometimes in harmony and sometimes in conflict:

	The teaching method employed		*The material content of the lesson*
1.	Same as before, *i.e.* direct teaching	with	same as before, *i.e.* formal work
2.	Same as before *i.e.* direct teaching	with	different from before, *i.e.* informal work
3.	Different from before, *i.e.* indirect teaching	with	same as before, *i.e.* formal work
4.	Different from before, *i.e.* indirect teaching which is guidance and suggestion, etc.	with	different from before, *i.e.* informal work which is creative, expressive and experimental.

Faced with so many movement permutations with regard to teaching method and material, it is not surprising that there still exists a great degree of confusion among students and teachers. The answer perhaps lies not only in what may seem to be the glib platitude of "it all depends on the individual needs of the class" but also in bearing in mind once more the requirements of the work which are creative and experimental —and in dance, expressive—ideas, and as high a standard of actual performance as is attainable. In order to achieve this the children need to think, do, feel and observe movement; and in order to help them to do so the development of the teacher's own teaching personality and the ability to observe and assess the individual needs of child and class is essential.

In helping children to work on movement lines the question arises as to whether or not to use themes for lessons. If you give themes, for example, shapes, turning and twisting, swing or time, you are in danger of placing children in a difficult situation by telling them what to do without telling them, for example, what "swing" or "time" is and how to cope with it, or giving them movement experience of it. In order to cope with themes like these children must have knowledge of the body awareness and spatial factor involved. It is of little value telling the children merely to make a long, thin shape or a symmetrical or asymmetrical shape—everyone has different ideas of what these are or could be. Surely it is better to emphasise the body awareness and spatial factor more clearly, by saying for example, "Can you get your legs close to one another but away from the rest of your body?" or "What different ways can you find of doing this?" or "How many?" Later one can bring in direct or indirect movement—indirect when you want a twist—but it should be clearly pointed out that there must be a change of body shape as well as pathway. In addition, to cope with themes successfully, children also need to be aware of the effort action required to cope with the apparatus—for example, pushing, pulling and recovery efforts and actions—and the concept of the purpose of loco-motion, for example, transference of weight.

The aim of teaching must not be purely to teach children the subject but to take ideas from the children in order to use what they contribute. Specialists with so much knowledge have to combine their knowledge with an observation of children before their work becomes really successful. Are children a means to an end or an end in themselves? Specia-list knowledge must guide and consolidate the work of children and their contribution to the lesson to its true end. Successful observation of children and their work must be a combination of child and movement observation. The aim should be to help children develop their own ideas, for their own and the teacher's combined satisfaction and achievement.

When working in the gymnasium two more problems arise concerned with the movement task—firstly the question of whether children should be graded according to their height, size and ability when working on apparatus. If this is done, however, it should be after a certain stage. This stage is reached when the teacher notices that more than one or two children are having difficulty in coping with the apparatus for various reasons. Also, children often grade themselves in groups, and therefore this could be allowed to happen as a matter of course and groups allowed to select their own apparatus on which to perform their own movement ideas. If all children have had comprehensive experience of all apparatus at simple stages, this could then lead to children working on apparatus on which they are supremely confident. It should be remembered that in the gymnasium there is always the element of the unfamiliar or what may, to a child, mean the unapproachable, and hence the element of fear.

In the author's opinion mere use of apparatus does not always dispel this, and neither does the teacher inciting the class to "be more courageous!"

The reasons for grading work on apparatus are for purposes of achievement—to ensure that there is no waste of time or discouragement on the part of the child. In addition it may well be a fallacy to presume that children do not go beyond their own ability for in actual fact they often do. Hence with grading there is less likelihood of accidents of a severe nature. An argument against grading is the problem of presenting the children with a sufficient challenge. We must be sure that this is done if grading is carried out. Also, the possibility of an improvement in work even if a child is weak on certain apparatus cannot be ignored. There can be no universal rule on this question. It is up to the individual teacher to know her class, their needs and capabilities, and to decide accordingly.

The most pertinent guide when setting apparatus tasks or confronting the children with apparatus can only be her knowledge of how children can master their bodies and the extent of their movement vocabulary on the floor.

The second problem arising is the question of supporting. Should this be allowed? In the author's opinion supporting is justified provided that the support helps to *support* the person's weight and does not *control* it for them entirely by lifting them over the apparatus acting as a crane or hoist. The children should also be aware of how to support and should be encouraged to use and to devise the most economical and suitable way; for example, which part or parts of the body to hold, where to stand in relationship to a moving body and how to move with the body or as the body moves in order to get continuity of movement.

MOVEMENT AS THE PRIMARY APPROACH TO PHYSICAL EDUCATION

Movement is where we go, with what, how we go and for how long. The use of movement as the primary approach to physical education is now accepted by many and has resulted in a great deal of successful and interesting work in many colleges, schools and education authorities. For many people, however, this method still presents insurmountable problems due to lack of understanding of what movement is, let alone how to use it.

Movement is the basis of physical education in so far that it must provide a movement vocabulary or the grammar of movement—that is, movement for movement's sake—in order to fulfil its separate tasks in dance and gymnastics. In dance movement is, however, only part of the problem as the main function of dance is to facilitate expression. Thus many other facets of the work are of equal if not of primary importance. Movement in itself cannot be the sole end-product of a dance lesson as the emphasis must surely be on the expressive and creative rather than on the purely physical side.

In gymnastics movement must be related and allied to apparatus to produce the mastery of movement on it which will result in physical skills. Movement plays a great part, and makes the most valuable contribution towards attaining confidence on apparatus. If a child has control of its body on the floor it can, with experience, apply the same control to apparatus, and a child is truly happy on apparatus only when it has achieved a skill and agility on it.

The basic factor which cannot be ignored is that movement training achieves the bodily control necessary for both gymnastics and dance, and to a certain degree for other braches of physical education. It must, therefore, surely be the starting point or initial impetus for any programme of work in physical education.

In movement education the children should be able to think, feel, do and observe movement in order to be able to use it as and when required. In *basic movement* it is used for a creative physical purpose—movement for movement's sake, locomotion for locomotion's sake. As has been said before, in *educational dance* movement is used for creative, expressive and physical purposes and for locomotion. In *educational gymnastics* it is used as creative physical movement for movement's sake but the emphasis is on locomotion *purpose* in order to meet the challenges of apparatus work.

It is the responsibility of the teacher to channel movement into various branches of physical education until the children understand the purpose of movement itself and can themselves apply it to all branches of physical education. Therefore in the initial stages, the teacher, by setting movement tasks, may have to channel the ideas of the children until they have reached the stage of awareness and recognition of the place of movement.

Confusion can arise when children do all branches of movement education, that is, basic movement and its application to educational gymnastics and dance, and in addition educational gymnastics and educational dance. On the floor children can produce movement which is basic to both gymnastics and dance and therefore will do so on apparatus. Do we wish to encourage or discourage this? In gymnastics children more gifted in dance can get more out of coping with the apparatus in this way than perhaps they would otherwise. In a dance lesson children more gifted in gymnastics, for example, those who tend to do acrobatic dance movement, can again get more out of the lesson than they would otherwise. Each child copes with the actual movement according to its individual talents, whether it is a dancer, a gymnast, or both, but in dance it must have expression in order to achieve the ultimate aim.

Children should have experience of the following creative movement:

1. *Basic movement.* This is a movement on the floor which is basic to both gymnastics and dance. It is movement for movement's sake so that the child can build up an all important movement vocabulary—the process of learning and acquiring the grammar of movement through an experimental, and explorative, creative process. Basic movement deals mainly with the following:

(*a*) *Where we go*, *i.e.* space (directions and levels).
(*b*) *With what*, *i.e.* body awareness.
(*c*) *How we go*, *i.e.* Time or Speed (quick, slow), Weight (heavy, light), Flow (free or arrested or bound).

2. *Basic movement into gymnastics.* This is movement on the floor and the apparatus. It is concerned with effort actions and movement factors, but the transitional movements as

well as the isolated or main actions are important. Basic movement uses physical skill and locomotion as a means to an end, but in this case the means is as important as the end itself. Basic movement into gymnastics deals with the following:

(a) The mastery of movement.

(b) Effort for effort's sake—transitional (preparatory or relaxation) as well as impact movement. It is a means to an end as well as an end in itself.

(c) Where we go, with what and how we go.

3. *Basic movement into dance*. This is movement on the floor with and without dictated rhythms. Locomotion and physical skill are used as a means to an end but are concerned mainly with rhythm, the movement factors and the movement elements. Basic movement into dance deals with the following:

(a) Rhythm and sound.

(b) The basic efforts.

(c) The movement elements.

4. *Educational gymnastics*. This is where locomotion and physical skill are used themselves as an end. Educational gymnastics is concerned with effort actions—the action in itself is the most important thing which by isolated, or main, or complete body movement reaches its climax in vaulting.

5. *Educational dance*. This is expressive movement which is an end in itself. Locomotion and physical skill in rhythmical and expressive work are, however, also important. Educational dance is concerned with creative and expressive movement in various dance situations.

One of the biggest problems is how to get the teachers and the children to understand and appreciate the differences between the above or, in other words, how to use movement in different ways for different purposes. One of the most pertinent problems for the majority is where the border-line between dance and gymnastics occurs. It has been said that confusion in the minds and therefore the teaching of students and teachers must inevitably lead to subsequent confusion in the minds and hence the movement of pupils. In gymnastics the emphasis is on achieving skill in the mastery of movement, and the ability of the child to meet the challenge that apparatus work presents. In dance the movement is a vehicle for the child's personality and qualities of expression. One might say, therefore, that dance is creative and expressive whilst gymnastics is creative only. The use of language to make contact with children and to stimulate movement must therefore be different as must the teaching approach. In gymnastics we use words descriptive of action, or words denoting action to produce actions; in dance we use expressive language to produce expressive movements.

The two branches of this modern work do meet in movement that is basic to both as has been shown previously, but this is concerned solely with floor work. In gymnastics the action, the shape and form of the body are important as we are concerned with skill on the floor and apparatus. Control of weight—that is weight transference and weight taking—is the largest part of movement mastery allied to body awareness, and training in the use of space in this work and basic movement training for gymnastics are concerned with this. In dance we are concerned with shape and form, rhythm and transportation using the movement factors, and movement elements and basic efforts in the various dance situations. The production of ideas and a movement vocabulary are, however, basic to both gymnastics and dance.

In gymnastics locomotion is with the hands and the feet (in order to obtain a vault or agility) whilst in dance locomotion is mainly with the feet. In gymnastics taking the weight on other parts of the body is usually for a transitional movement—a means to an end—whilst in dance this can be an end in itself. In gymnastics the effort action is stressed, for example, swing or push, whilst in dance the movement element action is stressed, for example, thrust or wring. When we jump in gymnastics we have a *take-off* into *flight* into *landing*—the jump being dependent on all combined factors. We must have a push and a landing—we must get on and off the apparatus or the floor. All factors are external, the one being converted into the other—the action being dependent upon what goes before and after. In dance we have either *impulse* (main effort) into *flight* into *glide* (fade-out) or *impact* which is to prepare and arrive (main effort). In dance a jump is an action sufficient to itself—we have the internal factor in that we can prepare inside ourselves. In gymnastics after a jump we have a recovery whilst in dance we have either a fade-out or a held position of arrival.

Continuity is also different in dance and gymnastics. In gymnastics one movement must lead directly into another in order to achieve a movement sequence whether on the floor or the apparatus. The finishing position of one movement can be the starting position of another, for example, leap-frog into forward roll into backward roll. In dance one movement dissolves into another and that other arises out of the previous movement.

Rhythm is used in gymnastics for purposes different from those in dance. In gymnastics rhythm is inside the child, and the child's own personal rhythm is governed by its own idea of speed with a feeling for what is quick and slow movement; or by the rhythm that the apparatus task dictates. Is it wise, in gymnastics, to state the speed at which children should move? Is not the important thing that this is the child's own personal decision when coping with apparatus, *i.e.* the speed at which it works on apparatus, provided that if it *means* to be quick it *achieves* speed and *moves* quickly? In dance, rhythm is again inside the child—its own personal rhythm— but is also governed by a record or a different rhythm required to stimulate movement.

THE PROBLEM OF TEACHER TRAINING

In order to cope with the task of modern physical education and the problems to which this gives rise, the training of teachers must be given great consideration. Are teachers trained to cope with the situation adequately? The problem besetting every teacher in service, at the present time, is one of coping with the needs of the class and keeping abreast of the current trends in physical education teaching (which change frequently) as conceived by inspectors, advisers or lecturers at college. In other words the problem is *how to get what they want* and *the results they want—the way you want* (or by your teaching methods) and *the results you want*—and at the same time to deal successfully with the individual needs of the class and the children. To achieve this immense, and what to inexperienced teachers may seem impossible, task, let us consider *what we all want*—which is two basic requirements—creative and expressive ideas and a high standard of performance both presented in an experimental and educational manner.

We can teach only what we know as the result of our training conditioned by the ideas of our own particular college, and our opinions and imagination. The scope of physical education teaching is therefore wide, varied and unlimited. The root of the matter, however, is not to cast aside your own training ideas or experience in favour of the current vogue or latest idea and to copy slavishly the exact method of demonstration, but to see what the aim is and fulfil it using *your method based upon your experience*; otherwise your class will merely be subjected to a series of different methods culled from different people in the profession, or a series of chapters swotted up from the latest book on physical education. Your aim is to make contact with the children as a teacher and a person, not as a physical education manual.

This touches upon what is to the author's mind one of the snags of physical education, and especially of movement teaching, namely, that different colleges have different methods—could not some means of generalisation be found? Also, so many students tend to teach "college method," whilst in actual fact their training should ensure that they are given not only knowledge, but also the scope within that knowledge to develop their own personal method of contact with children. It is, in the author's opinion, a dangerous presumption to assume that "with experience" a student will cease to deliver second-hand college lectures to children and begin to teach instead.

THE MOVEMENT SPECIALIST IN THE PRIMARY SCHOOL

In the author's opinion the movement specialist has a place in Primary school life. At the infant and junior stage children are most receptive, especially in movement education and its link with other aspects of their school life. Many children at this vitally important stage have to work to the limitations of the class teacher rather than to the extent of the teacher's capabilities and imagination. Primary school teachers today have a much wider curriculum to study and cover than in the past and many find certain aspects of this, especially movement, entirely beyond them. Whereas in the past it was possible for them to follow or digest a prescribed course and dictated syllabus this today no longer applies; and the aim of Primary movement education is not merely to play about or with the apparatus or to move to music without any stimulation, guidance and progression in the work. As a Primary school teacher it is vitally necessary in any form of physical education to create a learning situation by involving the class as participants, not merely to create solely a teaching situation where the class act as passengers.

It is often stated that this particular age group require the security of one teacher the whole time, and this may well apply to the infant reception stage, but today children are more confident than in the past and the structure of society demands that they become independent at an earlier age than before. Many mothers work and the child often spends a great deal of his time with other people before even coming to school and through his subsequent school life. Movement specialists are, or should be, people who have a wide knowledge of children as well as movement, who know how to apply one to the needs of the other and who have creative, lively personalities. Knowledge of children and personality are the most essential qualities when working with young children, and if in addition one possesses a knowledge of movement and its application to the needs of young children, one must surely be in a position to fulfil a need in Primary schools. Admittedly it may well be that experienced teachers are best fitted to cope with this situation, but some colleges are already beginning to realise this need in training movement or dance teachers for the junior and middle age-range in senior schools. One great advantage would be that there would arise some progression and continuity in movement education throughout the child's school life—how many teachers in Secondary schools refuse to tackle movement education or dance because the children lack previous experience? How many complain that they have to start at the beginning when a great deal of the initial creative urge has been lost or that the practical work is unsuited to the academic needs or maturity of a senior class due to its simplicity? Added to which one factor is overlooked—that is that due to the constant floating population of Primary teachers, many children in their early school life are consistently meeting and coping with new teachers. The hallmark of a good class and a good teacher is a happy, secure relationship and contact between teacher and child, and a good movement teacher is able to achieve this with any age range.

SYLLABUS PLANNING FOR SCHOOLS

Movement must develop the child's ability and willingness to follow guidance as well as his need for free invention and imagination. Thus our task is to enable children to experience movement over a wide field. In order to do this we must guide through suggestion, enable children to become aware of where we go, with what, how, and for how long we go. In a movement education programme, basic movement should include lessons on the discovery, awareness and use of the body, of space, weight, time and flow, in an imaginative and creative way. To sum up, the questions involved are as follows:

1. Have I got room to move?
2. In how many different directions can I move?
3. On how many different levels can I move?
4. At what speed do I move?
5. How do I move?
6. For how long do I move?
7. With what do I move?

In educational or creative dance opportunities should be provided for the following:

1. The development of basic movement into the art of dance.
2. Dramatic dance and dance mime.
3. Dance improvisation and composition.
4. Sound accompaniment and vocal sound including the use of vocal expression to stimulate movement.

In educational gymnastics opportunities should be provided for the following:

1. The development of basic movement into gymnastics on the floor and apparatus.
2. Lessons concerned with body awareness with regard to the floor and apparatus.
3. Lessons concerned with the use of space with regard to the floor and apparatus.
4. Lessons concerned with the use of weight control—the taking and transference of weight—with regard to the floor and apparatus.
5. Lessons concerned with the use of time and flow and the relationship of one to the other.
6. Lessons concerned with the instrumental use of the limbs, *i.e.* the legs are instruments to move the body from one place to another as hands and arms and other parts of the body can be used for locomotion.
7. Lessons dealing with a framework for apparatus use, for example, the different methods of arriving on, moving on, staying on or leaving apparatus by moving up, down, on, off, along, over, under, through, round it, etc., with special emphasis on shape, form and weight control.

Creative or educational games can be included in a movement programme of work if desired, as may also other arts subjects as creative activities. The inclusion of games, swimming, athletics and recreational pursuits, whether as part of the physical education programme or as extra curriculum or out-of-school activities, depends entirely upon the most economical and purposeful use of staff personnel and facilities, etc., and most important of all upon the needs and aptitudes of the children.

A syllabus should not be a rigid schedule which is followed slavishly year after year. Rather should it allow for adaptation and improvisation as the needs of the children, and particular classes and streams, change rapidly sometimes as they move or progress through the school—work which suited one fourth year admirably may well not suit or be applicable to the fourth year the ensuing year. Optional activities should, if at all possible, be included in the programme, especially with regard to senior pupils. After a certain time it is obvious as to whether or not a pupil is a hockey player, a gymnast or a dancer, and many problems of discipline arise solely due to the fact that the work is just not suited to the needs of the pupils. After a child has experienced and made an honest effort in a particular branch of the work but has failed to develop an interest, ability, enthusiasm or aptitude for it, from the child's point of view it is pointless to continue with this work. Children are not pieces to be moved about on a chess board in a game invented by adults, and if made to do so these days will rebel strongly. After they have left school children remember more how you treated them as people than what you taught them as a class, and many children who say they hate physical education often mean that they hate the teacher with a rigid and uncompromising attitude.

Physical education today is fulfilling its task in an educational, vocational and recreational way in various establishments, but whatever its place and task may be, people, be they adults or children, are still the basic factor and the work must be orientated towards this.

NOTE TO THE TEACHER

The remainder of the book is not intended to act as a rigid syllabus or merely as a curriculum but rather to illustrate what has been written previously. The underlying principle of method and aim should be noted. The examples given are the work of children whom the author has taught and are used to define and illustrate the application of the principle of method and aim, showing the results that can be achieved thereby.

It has been written in the particular format chosen, for, in the author's opinion, it is necessary not merely to illustrate "what to teach," but also "how to teach it." Theoretical ideas should also have practical application to the needs of children clearly illustrated, with the method of teaching progression also outlined. "The way in which it is taught" must, however, be the development of the teacher's own particular teaching personality. Theoretical ideas can be very helpful when purely descriptive but the best illustration of these ideas is either practical demonstration or illustrated written lesson example with emphasis on the teaching method. Much of the work may be said to be in note form rather than in flowing, descriptive sentences and paragraphs; but the former method is, after all, how one makes lesson plans and can be abbreviated further when so doing or in actual teaching. Also, we teach by using brief instructions or guidance, not by using long sentences, since when we reach the end of them, the children have either lost interest or their powers of concentration, or have lost sight of the original task or intention. The words "Stop" or "Rest" are still a more effective method of bringing the lesson to a halt, rather than the request to "Stop working, come down from the apparatus, sit comfortably on the floor and please listen for a minute, girls."

When considering the question (or problem) of teaching method and the presentation of material, a variety of approach is essential when dealing with both children and adults. When working with children the work should always be presented to them according to their particular age, ability and aptitude. When working with the student/teacher alternatives are possible. One can present the work to adults leaving the application to the child to the individual (indirect method), or one can present the work to them as if they themselves were the class of children (direct method).

At different times, therefore, one presents work to children and adults in a totally different way or in exactly the same manner.

To assist the reader, material addressed to the child is given throughout this book in the type-face as in Lesson One, p. 25. Material addressed to the teacher appears in the type-face used in this Note.

Chapter Two

BASIC MOVEMENT

MOTION FACTORS IN BASIC MOVEMENT

Basic movement is concerned with:

1. grammar of movement;
2. building up a movement vocabulary.

Figure 1 below illustrates the use of the motion factors in basic movement.

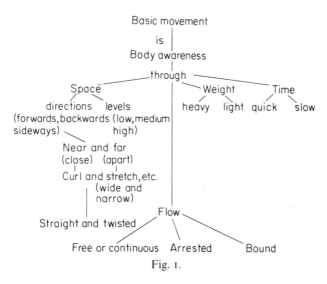

Fig. 1.

In basic movement the children should be encouraged to use different positions on the floor, in the air and with part of their body on the floor and part in the air.

In basic movement the factors to be considered are the motion factors of Space, Weight, Time and Flow, as classified by Laban.

23

1. *Space*—where the body can go or move:

(*a*) The discovery, awareness and use of space around the body when stationary and on the spot.

(*b*) The discovery, awareness and use of space about the spot and about the room.

(*c*) The difference between shapes and the variety of shape and form, *e.g.* narrow, wide, small, straight and twisted shapes.

(*d*) The discovery, awareness and use of different directions in space and different levels.

(*e*) The pathways of movement into space, *i.e.* direct and indirect or flexible movement, *e.g.* "snakes and ladders."

(*f*) The use of space by one child in relation to another child or children—either a partner or a group—or to other objects.

2. *Weight*—the discovery, awareness and use of strong and light movements performed by the whole or any part of the body.

3. *Time*—the discovery, awareness and use of quick (sudden) or slow or smooth (sustained) movements performed by the whole or any part of the body.

4. *Flow*—the discovery, awareness and use of the flow of movement:

(*a*) Movements which are continuous—which go on without pause or break and which could be called "free flow" or "over flow."

(*b*) Movements which come to a sudden stop and which could be called "arrested" or "frozen."

(*c*) Movements which continue or go on but are controlled and held, and which could be called "bound flow" or "controlled flow."

The principles to be considered in basic movement are therefore as follows:

1. The motion factors: space, weight, time and flow.

2. The six movement elements: strong, light, quick, sustained, direct, indirect.

It is vitally important to remember that without discovery first there can be no awareness and subsequently no use of the above factors of basic movement. Until a child has first discovered something it cannot be aware of that particular thing and hence is unable to make use of it. It is therefore important that the teaching method should follow an experimental progression of:

1. discovery,
2. awareness,
3. use.

If this pattern is not established children will experience difficulty in building up movement sequences or sentences.

BODY AWARENESS THROUGH SPACE, WEIGHT, TIME AND FLOW
(Lessons One to Five)

LESSON ONE

1. Walking about the room in a space:
   (a) *heavy,*
   (b) *light.*
2. Running about the room in a space:
   (a) *heavy,*
   (b) *light.*
3. Walking on *different parts of the feet, e.g. heels, toes, sides (inside and outside), balls of feet.* Now change to running on *different parts of feet.*
4. Walking about the room *light* thinking about a *space* followed by running about the room, *on toes, light* thinking about a *space.*
5. Walking about the room *light*, thinking about a *space,* with *feet together* and *feet apart.* Now do the same thing but run about the room.
6. In a *space* on the floor, on the spot, find different positions with *feet* apart—*stretching* them:

   (a) sitting, standing, kneeling, lying on:
      (i) *back,*
      (ii) *tummy or front* of body,
      (iii) *one side* of body,
      (iv) *the other side* of body,
   (b) *with hands and feet* on the floor or *combinations of this:*
      (i) *two hands, two feet,*
      (ii) *two hands, one foot,*
      (iii) *one hand, two feet,*
      (iv) *one hand, one foot* (all combinations of left and right).

Find different positions whilst doing the above, *e.g. tummy* facing floor, etc.

7. (a) Back to walking and running about the room, *light* on *toes,* thinking about being in a *space,* with *feet* apart.

(b) Moving about the room in any way you like with *feet* apart, then on *hands* and *feet* only and combinations of same with *feet* still apart.

8. Run about the room and jump through a *space* stretching *feet.*

9. How many ways can you find of getting your *feet near to,* and *far away* from the rest of your *body?*

10. Move about the room any way you like with *feet near to,* and *far away* from your *body.*

11. Get in the air with *feet near to,* and *far away* from your *body.*

12. On the spot try to get your *body* as *high* in the air and as *far away* from the ground as possible.

13. On the spot try to get your *body* as *close* to the floor as possible.

In this specimen lesson the body awareness and the motion factors are italicised in order to illustrate the build-up. The same build-up can be observed in ensuing work. It is vitally important that the teacher embarking upon this work should make sure the children understand what "being in a space" means. All too often we tell children to "find a space" without explaining what "space" is or means. To a child "being in a space" or "finding a space" means having plenty of room in front, behind him, at both sides of him, upstairs and downstairs.

LESSON TWO

1. Move about the room in any way you like:

(a) heavy,
(b) light,

thinking about being in a space.

2. Do the same as before but think about moving in different directions. How many can you find?

3. In a space, on the spot, on the floor, find different positions of taking weight on hands and feet, and combinations of same, getting feet together and apart, and near to, and far away from, the body.

4. Now move about the room taking and transferring weight as in (3) above.

LESSON THREE

1. Walking about the room:

(a) heavy,
(b) light.

2. Running about the room:

(a) heavy,
(b) light.

3. Walking and running about the room on different parts of feet.

4. Go back to walking and running about the room, thinking about being in a space.

5. Do the same as in (4) above but with feet together and then with feet apart.

6. In a space, on the spot, on the floor, find different positions to be in:

(a) with feet together (close to body),
(b) with feet apart (away from body).

For example, one can sit or stand, or do this with hands and feet on the floor, or with a combination of hands and feet on the floor.

LESSON FOUR

1. Move about the room taking your weight on your hands:

(a) heavy,
(b) light.

2. Move about the room taking weight on hands, light, thinking about moving in a space and in different directions.

3. On the spot, stretch your arms in different directions, adopt different body positions, getting arms near to, and far away from, your body as you stretch them.

4. Move your hand about in the space near to and away from your body trying to get your fingers near to and far away from the rest of your hand as you do this.

5. Run about the room, jump through a space. In how many different directions can you jump?

6. Make your whole body STILL, finding different ways of doing this in different positions, e.g. with feet on the floor.

7. Walk about the room quickly, stop STILL on the spot, and then FLOP.

8. Walk about the room quickly, stop STILL on the spot, and then GRIP with the body.

9. Do the same as in (7) and (8) above but walk about the room slowly.

LESSON FIVE

1. Move about the room in any way you like:

(a) heavy,
(b) light.

2. As before but concentrate upon moving in a space.

3. As before but move lightly and find different directions in space in which to move.

4. On the spot find as many different ways as you can of stretching and curling the body.

5. On the spot, how many different positions can you be in, whilst stretching your arms in as many different directions as possible?

6. In different positions shake different parts of your body, *e.g.* legs, head, etc., in different directions.

7. Run about the room lightly, jumping through as many different spaces as you can find, and in different directions.

BODY AWARENESS WITH EMPHASIS ON BODY PARTS
(Lessons One to Five)

LESSON ONE: Body parts

1. Shake the whole body:

    (*a*) with feet on the floor,
    (*b*) lying on the floor,
    (*c*) jumping in the air.

2. Rub, scratch, tickle different parts of the body:

    (*a*) against each other, *e.g.* elbow against elbow,
    (*b*) against other parts of the body, *e.g.* elbow against knee,
    (*c*) against the floor,
    (*d*) against a partner.

3. Shake and stretch different parts of the body, *e.g.* hands, elbow, head, close to and far away from the rest of the body.

LESSON TWO: Awareness of legs and arms

Find different ways and different positions to be in with arms and/or legs:

1. (*a*) close to one another,
    (*b*) close to the rest of body;
2. (*a*) far away from one another,
    (*b*) far away from the rest of body;
3. (*a*) close to one another,
    (*b*) far away from the rest of body;
4. (*a*) far away from one another,
    (*b*) close to the rest of body.

Different sequences can be made up from the above ideas.

LESSON THREE: The use of hands and feet

1. Move about the room using hands and feet—with different combinations of same—thinking about moving in different directions in space, on different levels, and with the body in different shapes.

2. On the spot, using hands and feet to support your weight, go from one position to another, and from there to yet another. Dissolving from one position to another is the transitional movement leading to the next held position or balance.

3. Fix about four ways or positions of balance moving from one into the other, etc., and repeat this sequence.

LESSON FOUR: Body awareness through shape in space

1. Move about the room taking your weight on your hands, thinking about space, directions and levels.

2. Same as (1) but now think about where your legs are with regard to one another, and the rest of the body, in terms of near and far.

3. On the spot stretch arms in different directions with the body in different positions.

4. Find different ways of:

    (*a*) getting fingers of hand near to, and far away from, body;
    (*b*) getting hand near to, and far away from, body;
    (*c*) getting leg or legs near to, and far away from, body.

5. Run about the room, jump through a space, using different directions to jump in, with legs:

    (*a*) near to/away from each other,
    (*b*) near to/away from rest of body.

6. On the spot find different positions in which to shake the body and then make it STILL in these positions.

LESSON FIVE: Body awareness through partner work

Contact with a partner can be obtained either by holding on to one's partner, or by resting on one's partner.

1. In a space away from partner, grasp one another:

    (*a*) feet with feet,
    (*b*) feet with hands,
    (*c*) hands with hands,
    (*d*) head with hands or feet,
    (*e*) seat with hands or feet,
    (*f*) body with hands or feet.

(*a*)–(*f*) can be done with one holding and one wriggling to get free. Different parts of the body can be used to hold and grasp with other than those mentioned above, *e.g.* elbows, knees, etc. This makes it a game and lends to it an element of fun which is very good especially for juniors.

2. With a partner work out positions in which one part, or parts, of the body are in contact with partner, and another part, or other parts, of the body are in contact with the floor *or* in the air.

3. With a partner work out positions in which one part, or parts, of the body are in contact with partner and with the floor, *and* in the air. The positions in (2) and (3) can be done with:

    (*a*) only one partner acting as the support and holding;
    (*b*) both the support and the active partner holding;

(*c*) only the active partner holding with the support remaining inactive in this respect;

(*d*) the support remaining inactive and the active partner merely resting on them.

The children must work for different positions of both partners, and for balance, grip and body tension, and for the perfection of body shape.

EXTENSION AND FLEXION THROUGH SPACE AND TIME
(Lessons One to Six)

LESSON ONE

This is primarily concerned with body shapes through curling and stretching the body on the floor and in the air.

1. Make sequences of (*a*)–(*d*) below, making curling and stretching shapes, with the body in different positions and in different places:

(*a*) Go from body on the floor in a curled shape to body off the floor in a stretched shape.

(*b*) Go from body on the floor in a curled shape to body with only feet on the floor in a stretched shape.

(*c*) Go from body on the floor in a curled shape to body on the floor in a stretched shape.

(*d*) Go from body with only feet on the floor, in a curled shape, to body with only feet on the floor, in a stretched shape.

2. Now progress to individual parts of the body, and do this, for example, with your hand on the floor and then off the floor, going from a curled to a stretched hand shape.

3. Now introduce the time element in activities (1) and (2) above, *e.g.* move from one position to another slowly, quickly, or from slow to quick and vice versa. Thus we begin to get the movement efforts of pushing, thrusting, etc., with our bodies.

LESSON TWO

1. On the spot and then moving about the room find different ways of going from:

(*a*) curl to stretch,
(*b*) stretch to curl,
(*c*) stretch to stretch,
(*d*) curl to curl.

2. Now make a movement sequence out of the above positions on the spot and then moving about the room.

LESSON THREE

1. Find different ways and different positions of stretching the body on the spot.

2. Move about the spot by bounding and stopping using leg gestures in space when you bound.

3. Move about the room bounding and stopping. Stretch the whole of your body on the spot where you stop.

4. Make up a sequence of bounding, stopping and stretching, varying the number of bounds, stops and stretches.

LESSON FOUR

1. Run about the room and jump through a space stretching and curling the body in the air.

2. In a space on the floor, on the spot, find different positions of going from curl to stretch, and from stretch to curl.

3. Move about the room doing this, working on the floor and in the air.

4. Now select four specific ways, fix this sequence and practise it on the spot and/or moving about the room. Hence we have now progressed to moving not only from one shape to another, but also from one spot to another, and from the floor into the air.

LESSON FIVE

1. Keeping the body or part of the body on the floor, curl with body low and then stretch with body high. Find different ways of doing this using different directions. Aim for continuity of movement.

2. Same as in (1) but get the body off the floor completely when you stretch.

3. Practise sequence (4) from Lesson Four.

LESSON SIX

1. On the floor stretch the body in different positions, *e.g.* sitting, standing, kneeling, lying, with weight on hands, etc.

2. In the air stretch the body to get different positions and shapes.

3. Now stretch the body in different ways and shapes with part of it on the floor and part in the air.

4. Make up a sequence stretching the body on the floor, then in the air, and then, with part on the floor and part in the air, arrange the sequence in order of personal preference.

The movements which result from this will generally be either "dance-like" or "gymnastic" movements or have a tendency towards acrobatic dance. The differentiation must be discussed with the children, especially with senior pupils, for the later development of these movements will be used for different purposes. Discussion may lead to the conclusion that "dance-like" movements, apart from being performed purely for shape and form and locomotion purposes, may later be put to music or used in response to some other external stimuli in dance, whilst "gymnastic" movements could be used on apparatus as a balance or for purposes of transference of weight, apart from shape and form and locomotion purposes in floor work.

5. Having fixed and practised sequence (4) above, now add variations, for example:

(*a*) use a shake as a transitional movement to get from one position of stretch to another;
(*b*) use a curling movement for transitional purposes;
(*c*) use a swing as a transitional movement;
(*d*) use a turn as a transitional or "in between" movement;
(*e*) vary the shape of your stretched movement, *e.g.* wide, narrow, or a combination of both.

6. Now bring in the time element if desired and if sufficient progress has been made, *e.g.* stretches and transitional movements can be done slowly, quickly, with sustainment, etc.

MOVEMENT EFFORTS AND THEIR COMBINATIONS
(Lessons One to Three)

LESSON ONE

1. On the spot, in different positions, *thrust* out different parts of the body in different directions.
2. Do the same thing but *push* out the different parts of the body.
3. As in (1) and (2) but start and finish in a curled position.
4. As in (1) and (2) but move about the room as you thrust and push body parts out into space.
5. Curl and stretch the whole body on the spot thrusting and/or pushing as you stretch, and curling slowly and quickly, *e.g.*:

(*a*) stretch by thrusting (quickly), curl slowly;
(*b*) stretch by pushing (slowly), curl quickly;
(*c*) stretch by thrusting (quickly), curl quickly;
(*d*) stretch by pushing (slowly), curl slowly.

6. Move about the room in any way you like, stop on the spot and thrust and/or push the whole or different parts of the body out into space.
7. Choose different parts of the body. Start with them close to the floor, then pull them up high sharply and then flop down. This is a "piece of elastic" idea—the idea of elastic being pulled out and then let go.
8. Roll and then shoot or thrust and/or push out different parts of the body, *e.g.* elbow, hand, etc.
9. Roll and then thrust or push out the whole of your body.

10. With a partner, curl up away from one another; reach out and touch one another with different parts of the body. Use thrusting and pushing efforts to do this. (The part or parts of your body not in contact with your partner must be as far away from them as possible.) Curl up and start all over again.

11. Same as (10) but alter your position each time you curl up and away from your partner to enable you to start again in a different position each time.

12. Move about the room in any way you like thrusting and/or pushing whilst moving.

LESSON TWO

1. Be "the toothpaste in the tube," and push or thrust or squiggle your way out. Make this into a sequence.

2. Start curled up in the tube and come out as before, and go back into the tube again. Find different positions and different ways to do this.

3. Now get out of the tube and back again continuously, combining your effort actions smoothly.

LESSON THREE

1. Using different directions and levels go about the room any way you like, then on the spot thrust and/or push the whole/different parts/the top half/the bottom half of body out.

2. On the spot, curl and stretch whole body in different directions, on different levels, moving slowly and quickly, using pushing and thrusting efforts to stretch.

3. On the spot make a sequence of pushing, thrusting and squiggling movements with a starting and a finishing position.

In this work on movement efforts, the efforts which can be used are, for example:

Thrusting — quick and direct

Pushing   — slow and direct

Gliding   — slow and direct

Dabbing   — quick and direct

Wringing   — slow and indirect

Slashing   — quick and indirect

Floating   — slow and indirect

Flicking   — quick and indirect

It is better to deal with efforts separately in the initial stages and then combine them together in sequences. Here we have a strong tendency for the movement to lead into dance.

CONTROL OF WEIGHT
(Lessons One to Four)

Control of weight through body awareness and space
(*Lessons One to Three*)

LESSON ONE

1. Move about the room walking, running, moving high/low, transferring weight from:

   (*a*) one foot to the other;
   (*b*) two feet to two feet;
   (*c*) one foot to two feet;
   (*d*) two feet to one foot.

2. On the spot take your weight on different parts of the feet and *balance* there:

   (*a*) on one foot, *e.g.* heels, toes;
   (*b*) on both feet; *e.g.* heels, sides of feet.

3. Move about the room transferring your weight from one part of your feet to other parts, *e.g.* from toes to heels, etc.
4. On the spot take your weight on different parts of the body and *balance* there, *e.g.* head and hands, seat, etc.
5. On the spot transfer your weight from one body part to another/other body parts, *e.g.* from hands to feet, feet to seat, etc. Find different ways of doing this adopting different body positions.
6. Fix a weight transference sequence from the above, aiming for continuity, and at the end of this sequence put in a balance or held position.
7. Move about the room transferring your weight from one part to another/other body parts, *e.g.* hands to feet. Aim for continuous movement all the time. Fix a sequence.

LESSON TWO

1. On the spot take your weight on to different parts of the body, in different positions, *e.g.* sitting, standing, kneeling, lying, etc.
2. On the spot take your weight on to different parts of the body as before, then transfer your weight on to another part/other parts of the body and continue doing so.
3. On the spot take weight as before but balance there in a held position before transferring the weight as before.

4. Take your weight on to part or parts of the body and balance there; move about with your weight on this particular part or in this position and then roll.

5. Take your weight on to part or parts of the body, balance there, then move about transferring your weight on to another part of the body.

This lesson can be applied specifically to apparatus, in a basic movement into gymnastics lesson, as follows:

1. On apparatus take your weight on different parts of the body in different positions.

2. Take your weight as before but then transfer it and keep on doing so.

3. As before but balance in a held position in between each transference of weight.

4. Take your weight, balance there, then move on, along or off the apparatus with your weight on this particular part, and finish the sequence with a roll.

5. Take your weight, balance there, then move on, along or off the apparatus transferring your weight on to another part or other parts of the body as you do so.

Suitable apparatus can be:

(a) forms;
(b) forms inclined on ribstalls (wallbars);
(c) ribstalls;
(d) held knotted or single ropes;
(e) bars, single or double on narrow or broad edge;
(f) box;
(g) horse.

LESSON THREE

1. On the spot, take your weight on different parts of the feet. Transfer your weight from part or parts to another part or other parts of feet.

2. Do this moving about the room, *e.g.* walking, running, etc.

3. This taking of weight and subsequent transference of weight, either on the spot or about the room, can now be done using hands, feet and legs, hands and arms, trunk, specific parts of trunk or a combination of body parts. In this lesson, therefore, the body parts that can be used are as follows:

(a) Feet—one or both.
(b) Hands—one or both.
(c) Feet and legs—one or both.

(*d*) Hands and arms.
(*e*) Trunk—back, front or sides of body.
(*f*) Specific parts of trunk:

(*i*) Back of body, *e.g.* seat, the back itself, shoulders and back of head, back and shoulders and back of head. The arms may be used in addition to help support weight.

(*ii*) Front of body, *e.g.* tummy, tummy and thighs or legs, chest. Arms may again be used to support weight.

(*iii*) Sides of body, *e.g.* chest, waist, waist and thighs or legs. Arms may again be used to support weight.

(*g*) Combination of body parts:
(*i*) hands and feet,
(*ii*) hands, feet and legs,
(*iii*) hands, arms and feet,
(*iv*) hands, arms, feet and legs,
(*v*) hands and trunk or specific parts of trunk,
(*vi*) feet and trunk or specific parts of trunk,
(*vii*) hands, arms, feet and trunk or specific parts of trunk,
(*viii*) hands, feet, legs and trunk or specific parts of trunk,
(*ix*) hands, arms, feet, legs and trunk or specific parts of trunk.

As before this lesson can be applied specifically to apparatus, in the basic movement into gymnastics lesson, using forms, bars, box, ropes and ribstalls.

Control of weight in movement sequences

LESSON FOUR

1. On the floor, on the spot, make up a movement sequence containing a jump, a roll and an agility (an acrobatic movement performed on or along the floor), and/or a balance or held position.

2. Now make up a movement sequence containing the above but move about the room doing it. This can either be the identical sequence performed on the spot or it can be a different one.

As before, this lesson can be applied specifically to apparatus, in the basic movement into gymnastics lesson.

In Lessons 1–4 on control of weight the stress should be on using as many different parts of the body as possible. The balance factor or "held position" factor in this work can be of either primary or secondary importance according to the needs and/or ability of the class. The danger, with less experienced or gifted movers, is that loss of continuity of movement can occur if the "held" balance factor is over-stressed.

MOVEMENT FACTORS OR EFFORT ACTIONS
(Lessons One to Four)

LESSON ONE: Jumps

1. Jump on the spot and about the room transferring your weight as follows:

   (*a*) from two feet to two feet,
   (*b*) from two feet to one foot,
   (*c*) from one foot to one foot (same or different),
   (*d*) one foot to two feet.

2. Jump high, jump low on the spot and about the room. Jump in different directions.

3. On the spot make up three jumps:

   (*a*) without pause,
   (*b*) with pause (going down to full knees bend).

4. On the spot repeat your jump sequence but make your feet either close to or away from your body.

5. Now think about how the shape of the rest of your body can fit in with your feet as you perform your jump sequence.

6. Now make your jump sequence take you about the spot using different directions, as well as levels.

7. Find ways of jumping high and landing or finishing low using different directions.

8. Find ways of jumping low and landing high or finishing high using different directions.

9. Now think about making different shapes, *e.g.* wide, narrow, curled or tucked, as you jump and land or finish, using different directions and different levels.

10. Make up a sequence of take-off into flight into landing using different directions and levels, and different body shapes for the jump. A balance or held position can be added at the end of the sequence if desired.

LESSON TWO: Swings

Find different ways of swinging a partner using different body holds as follows:

   (*a*) Arms:

   (*i*) arms holding arms,
   (*ii*) arms holding neck,
   (*iii*) arms holding waist and hips,
   (*iv*) arms holding legs.

   (*b*) Hands holding hands.
   (*c*) Legs and/or feet:

(*i*) legs holding neck,
(*ii*) legs holding waist,
(*iii*) legs holding legs.

(*d*) A combination of any of the above.

In this work either one partner or both partners can do the holding for the swings. It is important to point out the necessity for body swing in order to get impetus and flight— merely to lift the partner off the floor is not sufficient. One must also point out the necessity for the "swung" body to have a position, grip, tension and balance whilst being swung —to lie limp and soggy will only impede the partner. It is necessary that the children should work out the amount of swing to be achieved by one partner or both partners in order to make the activity successful.

LESSON THREE: Discovery of movement factors or effort actions in control of weight

These factors are as follows:

> pushing from, off or against;
> swinging;
> pulling;
> a combination of the above.

1. Using different body parts, *e.g.* hands, feet, etc., move from low to high and from high to low positions on the floor, *e.g.* crouch jump to handstand to crouch jump. Find different ways of doing this.

2. Find different ways of getting your body off the floor into the air, *e.g.* push yourself off the floor, swing your body into the air, etc. Can you change direction in the air? Here we tend to get jumps.

3. Make up a sequence combining the tasks in (1) and (2).

4. On the spot find different ways of balancing or holding positions where some part or parts of the body are in contact with the floor. Can you discover which positions need a "resting" contact with the floor and which need a "resisting" contact in order to maintain balance?

5. Go back to your sequence in (3) adding a balance or held position at some point. Find different ways of getting from position of balance, into transference of weight, into position of balance, into flight in the air, etc.

6. How many different sequences can you find?

LESSON FOUR: Use of movement factors or effort actions in control of weight

1. On the spot find ways of transferring your weight from one part of the body to another without altering your original position a great deal, for example:

(a) crouch jump, into handstand, into elbow stand, into a glide or sink on to chest or front of body;

(b) crouch jump, into handstand, into flip flap movement on to feet;

(c) backward roll, into handstand on to feet, into standing position.

2. Do the same movement tasks as in (1) but interrupt the continuous flow of movement to hold a position or to balance at some point, *e.g.* crouch jump, into handstand balance (or held position), into flip flap movement or spring on to feet.

3. Now add on the impetus of a run or flight to the above movement tasks with or without a held or balance position, for example:

(a) dive or run or jump into crouch jump, into handstand (with or without balance), into flip flap movement or (handspring) on to feet,

(b) run into handspring on to feet.

The above are only examples. The general principle itself must be followed to enable children to create in various ways. As before, this work can be applied specifically to apparatus in the basic movement into gymnastics lesson. It is from the latter work that we get or begin to get agilities and vaults, for example, using the box we can get flight from the floor, into astride sitting on the box, into swing into handstand (with or without balance), and continue off with a flip flap movement, or handspring on to feet.

BODY ALIGNMENT

In basic movement lessons and in the application of basic movement to dance or to gymnastics the question of body alignment must arise. It is a good plan to encourage children to think about body alignment as they move, whether on the spot or about the room, and when making different body shapes. It is a mistake, however, to lead them to think of aligning their head and neck with only one part or one side of the body. The head and neck in movement can be in alignment with the trunk (upper or lower part) or the appendages, *i.e.* arms and legs, or the right or left side of the body. We can have either linear or straight alignment, or alignment which is curved or is an extension of a body curve.

SYMMETRY AND ASYMMETRY

This is a further question which arises in basic movement and in its application to the various branches of physical education. If symmetry and asymmetry is to be taken as a theme for a lesson—as it is by some—it is advisable for both the teacher and the class to be aware of the digressions from true symmetry and asymmetry in order to prevent confusion in the minds and hence movement of the pupils. It is not, in the author's opinion, sufficient to define the question of symmetry and asymmetry in terms of body shape alone. The factor of weight control and weight distribution must be taken into account. Whether the body weight is being taken and held in a static position, or is being transferred (immediately or delayed), two possibilities are apparent. We can have symmetry of body shape with either equal or unequal distribution of weight throughout the body, or asymmetry of shape with equal or unequal distribution of weight throughout the body.

There is also the question of symmetry and asymmetry of shape when passing out of the plane of symmetry, for example, when moving in a sideways direction in a jump (extension or tuck) with a symmetrical or asymmetrical shape, with equal or unequal distribution of weight.

In addition there is the question of movements which in terms of body shape and weight distribution pass from asymmetry, to symmetry, back to asymmetry, with an' unequal weight distribution, to equal weight distribution, back to unequal weight distribution. Examples of this are a cartwheel and a roll (extension or tuck). A cartwheel alters in shape and weight distribution during its performance. A sideways roll, whilst altering in weight distribution, may not alter in shape but passes at some point out of the plane of symmetry.

Therefore a *wholly* symmetrical movement is where both sides of the body are making the same shape, and where the weight is equally distributed throughout the body or both sides of it, and where movement is confined wholly to the plane of symmetry. If shape only is to be considered, a symmetrical movement is one where both sides of the body are making the same shape, and an asymmetrical one where one side of the body is in a different shape from the other side, regardless of weight distribution or whether or not the body stays all the time in the plane of symmetry while moving.

Chapter Three

BASIC MOVEMENT INTO EDUCATIONAL DANCE

When planning a lesson which concerns the application of basic movement to dance or gymnastics, one must decide what is the important or main factor of the lesson and achieve this through two other subsidiary or derivative factors. A third or incidental factor can also be involved or used if desired. The main factor, for example, body awareness, is achieved through subsidiary factors, for example, any two of the following—Time, Flow and Weight—with the additional or incidental factor of Space.

Basic movement into dance is concerned with using the grammar of movement or a vocabulary of movement built up in basic movement lessons in terms of the direct application of body awareness and space to time (rhythm), weight (effort) and flow (duration of movement).

BODY AWARENESS USING SPACE AND TIME
(Lessons One and Two)

LESSON ONE

1. Using different positions, *e.g.* lying on the floor, with feet on the floor or in the air, shake the whole body.

2. Shake different parts of the body, *e.g.* head, elbow, hand, etc. Use different directions and levels to do this. Also think about shaking the chosen body parts near to or far away from other body parts.

3. Find out in how many different places you can put different parts of the body, *e.g.* how many different places can you find in which to move your hand? If possible *watch* the body part this is moving.

4. To a given or dictated rhythm (quick and/or slow) on a drum use different parts of the body to start low, and pull up high, and then flop down low again. The starting position can either be close to the floor or close to another part of the body.

5. Now choose and fix a sequence using three specific body parts to work as in (4).

LESSON TWO

1. Using hands (one and then both) shake and stretch them in space (quickly and/or slowly).

2. Using feet (one and then two) shake and stretch them in space (quickly and/or slowly).

3. To a dictated drum rhythm (quick and/or slow) start in any position with your elbow close to the body. Now stretch it out away from the body into space and bring it back in again close to the body. Use different directions and different levels and different body parts to do this. The rhythm used can be slow for stretching out and quick for coming in again, or vice versa.

4. Working on the floor and in the air, using different directions and levels to get different body positions, tuck the whole body in and then stretch it out as far as possible. Again the rhythm used can be either quick or slow.

5. Start in a curled shape with knees tucked up to head. In this position roll and roll and roll and then stretch out quickly on the spot. Find different directions in which to roll and different directions, levels and shapes for stretching movements.

6. To a dictated drum rhythm running, leaping and then stretching on the spot, *e.g.* run, run, run, leap and stretch. For a variety of movement leap in different directions, and make different shapes in the air when you leap. The stretch on the spot after landing can be done slowly or quickly in different directions and on different levels.

BODY AWARENESS USING WEIGHT AND TIME

1. On the spot, shake legs in the air and then stamp your feet on the floor. Establish a rhythm of your own. Find different places (directions and levels) and different positions in which to do this.

2. Travel about the room then jump and shake legs in the air. On landing stamp feet on the floor, on the spot. Again establish a rhythm of your own to do this.

3. On the spot using arms—shake them in the air then beat out a rhythm with hands on the floor. Use different aspects of space (directions and levels).

4. Pick different parts of the body to shake in the air and beat on the floor, establishing a rhythmical sequence using strong and light efforts, quick and slow rhythms.

5. Moving on the spot and about the room make up a sequence using different body parts and different efforts and rhythms. Sequences which can be used are, for example:

    (*a*) shake and stamp,
    (*b*) shake and stretch (push or thrust),

with different weight and time elements.

Thus in this lesson we have body awareness using weight and time with space as the incidental factor.

BODY AWARENESS USING WEIGHT AND FLOW

Using different directions and working on different levels make up a sequence using different efforts (strong and light), and different rhythms (quick and slow), using movements which continue for a different duration of time (movements without pause and movements which come to a sudden halt or stop). Suggested effort sequences are as follows:

(a) Squiggle (or squeeze) leading into stretch movements. According to the time and weight element used the squiggle may be either a wring or a flick leading into a push or a thrust for the stretch.
(b) Squiggle (or squeeze) leading into stretch movements. According to the time and weight element used the squiggle may be either a float or a slash leading into a glide or a dab for the stretch.
(c) Stretch leading into squiggle movements can be treated in the same way as in (a) and (b).

In the author's opinion it is wise to encourage children, at this stage, to think about basic efforts in terms of time (quick, slow) and weight (strong, light), and space (direct, indirect), rather than by teaching them the exact terminology of wring, flick and dab, etc. To refer to movements as squiggles and stretches which are indirect and direct and which can be either quick or slow, or strong or light, etc., will result in wrings and thrusts of their own accord without cluttering up children's minds with excessive and, at this stage, unnecessary terminology which for them may have no meaning or may merely confuse the issue and cloud the movement.

STRETCH IN DANCE USING FLOW
(Lessons One and Two)

LESSON ONE

1. Make up a sequence where the body is in three positions of stretch—one on the floor, one in the air, and one with part of the body on the floor and part in the air. Put them in any order according to individual preference and repeat sequence when fixed.
2. Now put a turn in between each position of stretch as a transitional movement to aid continuity. We therefore have a sequence of

number one turn, into number one position of stretch, into number two turn, into number two position of stretch, into number three turn, into number three position of stretch, and repeat.

The turns and stretches can be done thinking in terms of space (in different directions and on different levels), shape (narrow, wide or curled) and time (quick or slow).

LESSON TWO

In this lesson a dance composition can be created using the sequence consisting of turning and stretching movements created in the previous lesson. The record "Moon River" (Mercer and Mancini) is a useful piece of music for this purpose. The following build-up of the dance is illustrated as follows:

1. In groups of four number off 1–4. Start in a position of stretch with group relationships. After the first bar of introductory music when the main tune or theme begins, using your first turn, into first position of stretch, move out of the group in sequence 1–4 one after the other.

2. Using your second turn and second position of stretch move back into the group in sequence 1–4 one after the other.

3. Using your third turn and third position of stretch all move out of the group together.

4. Move about the room repeating your own individual turning into positions of stretch sequence.

5. When the vocal part begins move towards a partner and work out a sequence of turning into positions of stretch together.

6. All end in a position of stretch to finish.

Thus in order to arrive at dance from a basic movement application we have to:

(a) work at the body movement first, allowing room for individual experimentation and creative ability,

(b) harness it to rhythm, sound or music,

(c) create movement patterns for the individual, for the individual in relationship to a partner or a group.

BASIC MOVEMENT INTO ATHLETICS

This can most easily be illustrated by giving example of a specimen lesson dealing with a particular skill, for example, the western roll.

1. Experimental work jumping over canes in as many different ways as possible.

2. Now work on different combinations of take-off and landing, for example:

Take-off		Landing
from two feet	to	two feet,
from one foot	to	two feet,
from two feet	to	one foot,
from one foot	to	one foot, etc.

3. The take-off must be from one foot and the landing must be on that same foot. Try using both right and left foot for this purpose.

4. Having established the foot chosen for take-off and landing purposes, find out in how many different directions you can face on landing.

5. Experiment in landing with different parts of the body facing the floor or mat in different positions.

6. Experiment in landing and taking weight on different parts of the body.

Then one must teach the particular skill required for the particular athletic event. In athletics and games we are concerned with teaching a particular skill that has to be acquired, but with an experimental approach to a directed activity. This experimental approach is concerned with body awareness (the instrumental and most economical use of the limbs), with space (the path or direction of the body in space and the positioning of it in relation to the limbs), and with the use of weight or effort actions in order to acquire a particular skill.

BASIC MOVEMENT INTO GAMES

Here again a specimen lesson is used to illustrate a skill (for example, dribbling and driving in hockey).

1. Get the ball from one side of the field to the other using the stick any way you like. Use various parts of the stick to make contact with the ball. Which do you find is the best part to use?

2. This time try to keep the stick as close to the ball as possible as you take it across the field. Experiment with hands on the stick close together, far apart, etc. Which hand do you find goes on top and which underneath? Whereabouts on the stick do you put your hands? What action do you use—a tap or a "wham" to keep the stick close to the ball?

3. Use the same ideas as before, but this time try to get the ball as far away from the stick as possible as you take it across the field. Ask yourself the same questions with regard to the positioning of the hands on the stick and action or effort force required.

By this means of questioning and experimentation it has been found that children will generally arrive at the correct conclusion or solution to the problem of the particular skill required with regard to the positioning of hands on the stick, etc. Having discovered it for themselves children will tend to remember and retain it longer than if they had simply been told it in the very first instance. From this basis we then go on to teaching the more complicated points of the particular games skill. There is still a wide area to be explored in creative games and in this particular field Laban's movement principles will be of far greater value than in the field of the more traditional and accepted school games, which are essentially competitive, and which, as they are played to defined and specific rules and regulations, in defined and specific areas with certain boundaries, and with a defined and specific aim—e.g. the scoring of goals—necessitate a defined and specific way of playing and controlling the particular game. The use of body awareness, space, positioning and the ability to work not only as an individual but as part of a team are, however, fundamental movement skills.

Chapter Four

BASIC MOVEMENT INTO EDUCATIONAL GYMNASTICS

This is concerned primarily with the direct application of the grammar of movement and the vocabulary of movement to control of weight, *i.e.* the taking and transference of weight, their combination and how one leads into the other, and their application to agility work as illustrated in Lessons One to Ten below. It is also concerned with this control of weight on the floor and apparatus with regard to body awareness, space and flow as illustrated in Lessons Eleven to Seventeen.

WEIGHT TAKING (STATIONARY BALANCE)
(Lessons One to Three)

LESSON ONE

1. On the ribstalls or wallbars balance in different positions, with hands (one or two) on the floor, and with the rest or part of the body on the ribstalls and/or part of the body in the air.

2. Now think about legs being near to and far away from the rest of the body as you balance in the above positions in (1).

3. Now think about legs being near to and far away from one another as you work in (1).

4. On the spot find different positions of balancing with hands and feet on the floor, for example:

    (*a*) with two hands and one foot in contact with the floor,
    (*b*) with two feet and one hand on the floor,
    (*c*) with one hand and one foot (same or opposite) on the floor,
    (*d*) with two feet and two hands on the floor.

5. As in (4) but with legs near to and far away from the rest of the body and one another.

LESSON TWO

1. With weight on hands on the floor, and with the rest of body on the ribstalls, or with part of the body on the ribstall and part in the air, find different ways of balancing with:

    (*a*) legs close to and away from body,
    (*b*) legs close to and away from one another,
    (*c*) body close to and away from the ribstall.

2. Find different ways of balancing on the floor with weight on hands and feet.

3. Find different ways of balancing on the floor with weight on one hand and one foot. Choose three positions.

4. Move about the room any way you like, then on the spot balance in the first position chosen in (3) above. Travel again, then on the spot balance in the second position chosen above, travel again and then on the spot balance in the third position chosen above.

LESSON THREE

1. Balance on a partner, in a position of stretch, with or without holding on to them. You may be entirely on your partner's body or part of you may be in contact with their body and part of you in the air.

2. As before, but this time your partner may assist you to balance by holding you.

3. Now find ways of balancing with part of your body on your partner and part on the floor, and/or part in the air. Your partner may hold you to assist balance if required.

WEIGHT TRANSFERENCE (CONTINUOUS BALANCE)
(Lessons Four and Five)

LESSON FOUR

1. Transfer your weight from seat to feet and back again.

2. As you do this work from the low to the high level.

3. On the spot transfer your weight as before, but when you come up on to your feet move about the spot with a jump, transferring weight from feet to feet, and then repeat the sequence.

4. As you do this stretch the body, either as you:

    (*a*) get up on to feet, or
    (*b*) when your are up with weight on feet, or
    (*c*) as you jump about the spot.

5. Now bring in the time element and make your body stretch with either quick or slow movements or both.

LESSON FIVE

  1. On the spot transfer your weight from:

    (*a*) feet to feet,
    (*b*) feet to hands,
    (*c*) a combination of (*a*) and (*b*).

Find different ways of doing this.

  2. Now work on different levels as you do this—sometimes high, sometimes low, etc.

  3. Moving about the spot transfer your weight from feet to hands to feet again as in a cartwheel.

  4. On the spot transfer your weight from feet to hands to feet again in different ways. Choose one way and practise this.

  5. Now combine (3) and (4), *i.e.* transference of weight moving about the spot and transference of weight on the spot. This is also the combination of one set and one chosen or free choice transference of weight.

  6. Vary the number of times you repeat each transference of weight to make a continuous sequence, *e.g.* three cartwheels travelling about the spot or about the room, and one free choice transference of weight on the spot or vice versa.

  7. Now combine this sequence of transference of weight about the spot or about the room, and on the spot with a balance on the ribstalls or some other piece of apparatus. Thus we get transference of weight from floor to apparatus and back to floor again. We can, for example, transfer our weight moving along the floor in a cartwheel, into a handstand on the spot, into a reverse hanging balance on the ribstalls, and back to the floor again.

  8. Vary this move away from the apparatus back to the starting point of your sequence by transference of weight, either by the same sequence which was used to approach the apparatus or by a different one.

From this work on weight taking and weight transference it should be possible for the child to deduce that one can take one's weight and hold it in a position of stationary balance on the spot on floor or apparatus; and that one can transfer one's weight, in continuous balance, on the spot or moving about the spot, or moving about the room, and also in order to get from floor to apparatus and back to the floor again. One should then progress to the combination of weight taking and weight transference and the question of how one leads into the other.

THE COMBINATION OF WEIGHT TAKING AND WEIGHT TRANSFERENCE
(Lessons Six to Nine)

This is concerned with:

1. weight taking, *i.e.* stationary balance,
2. weight transference, *i.e.* continuous balance,
3. weight transference into weight taking, *i.e.* continuous balance into stationary balance,
4. weight taking into weight transference, *i.e.* stationary balance into continuous balance.

LESSON SIX

1. Move about the room, *e.g.* walking, running, etc., moving high and low, transferring your weight from:

    (*a*) one foot to the other,
    (*b*) two feet to two feet,
    (*c*) one foot to two feet,
    (*d*) two feet to one foot.

2. On the spot take your weight on a different number of feet and using different parts of feet, and balance there, *e.g.* on one foot, both feet, on toes, on heels, etc.

3. Moving about the room transfer your weight from part or parts of the feet to another part or other parts of the feet.

4. On the spot take your weight on different parts of the body and balance there. Adopting different positions now transfer your weight from one part or parts of the body to another part or other parts of the body and balance there, taking or holding your weight in between each transference of weight. Thus we have weight transference in between each weight taking.

5. Move about the room transferring your weight from one part or parts of the body to another or other parts, *e.g.* from hands to feet, feet to feet, etc.

LESSON SEVEN

1. Find four positions of taking weight and balancing there with:

    (*a*) legs close to body and to one another,
    (*b*) legs away from body and away from one another,
    (*c*) legs close to body and away from one another,
    (*d*) legs away from body and close to one another.

As you do this, think about adopting different positions, *e.g.* sitting, lying, etc., and also think about which parts of the body are taking weight and which parts are in the air.

2. Combine the above four positions chosen so that you can move from one position to the next position:

(*a*) without radically altering your position,

(*b*) by putting in a transference of weight in between each stationary balance. This transference of weight can be done on the spot or done to move you to a different spot where you can go into the next position of stationary balance.

LESSON EIGHT

1. On the ribstalls balance in different positions with part of your body on the floor, part on the ribstall and part in the air.

2. As you do this experiment get legs near to and far away from one another and the rest of the body.

3. Transferring your weight on to different parts of the body, get up to, balance on and get away from the ribstall. When in position of balance on the ribstall either the whole or part of the body may be in contact with it.

LESSON NINE

1. Transfer your weight from the floor on to the ribstall, balance there and transfer your weight from the ribstall back on to the floor. Find different ways of doing this.

2. Using forms and mats in addition to the ribstall (Fig. 2), transfer your weight from the form to the mat, then on to the ribstall and balance there, and then transfer your weight from the ribstall back on to the mat or floor. This activity or task can be either purely experimental and/or set, *e.g.* extension jump from the form on to mat, etc.

3. After coming off the ribstall continue the transference of weight back on to the mat and from there on to the form so you arrive back at the beginning of the sequence.

Apparatus plan

 Ribstall

 Mat

———————— Form

Fig. 2.

CONTROL OF WEIGHT INTO AGILITIES

LESSON TEN

1. Using different directions roll with legs bent and stretched in symmetrical and asymmetrical body shapes.

2. Find different ways of balancing with feet close to head. Now move about the spot or the room either by:

(*a*) transferring your weight to other parts of the body, or
(*b*) by maintaining the same body position.

Examples of (*a*) are as follows:

(*i*) Position of prone lying on stomach with feet to head, hands holding ankles or propping weight on the floor. Now transfer weight from this position on to knees and feet and continue backwards into a backward roll.

(*ii*) Crouch or curl position lying on back with feet close to head. Now come up on to feet into forward or backward roll.

(*iii*) Position of elbow, head and hands, or handstand with feet close to head. Now come up on to feet either forwards or backwards so we get these various body-part stands leading into crab or forward roll on to feet, etc.

Examples of (*b*) are as follows:

(*i*) Position of prone lying on stomach with hands holding ankles with feet to head. Now roll sideways keeping in this position.

(*ii*) Crouch or curl position, lying on back, with feet close to head and hands holding ankles. Now roll sideways keeping in this position.

(*iii*) Position of elbow, head and hands, or hand, stand with feet close to head. Keeping in this position move forwards, backwards and sideways.

3. Find ways of taking your weight on one part of the body, transferring it to a different part or parts in order to travel, and finish at the end of the sequence with weight on yet another body part, for example:

(*a*) handstand into forward roll on to feet,
(*b*) Chinese handstand into backward roll on to feet.

How much of the above work can be applied to apparatus will depend upon the amount of skill gained in floorwork, experience of apparatus work and the courage of the individual child.

CONTROL OF WEIGHT WITH REGARD TO BODY AWARENESS,
SPACE AND FLOW
(Lessons Eleven to Seventeen)

LESSON ELEVEN

1. Move about the room taking weight on hands moving in a space and in different directions.

2. Now move with legs close to, and away from the body, with legs together or apart.

3. Get over mats with weight on hands thinking about moving in different directions with legs close to and away from one another, and close to and away from the rest of the body. Fix one way and practise it.

LESSON TWELVE

1. Get over the mat without touching it with your body, moving in different directions.

2. As you do this try to stretch legs as far away from one another, and as far away from the rest of the body, as possible.

3. In a space on the floor find different ways of stretching legs. Take your weight on different parts of the body to do this.

LESSON THIRTEEN

1. Get over mats in different ways thinking about moving in different directions, on different levels and with body in a variety of shapes. Aim for continuity of movement in the sequence of getting up to, over, and away from the mat. The transference of weight used to get up to, over, and away from the mat can be the same throughout the whole sequence or it can be varied.

2. In a space on the floor find different ways of moving from one shape to another, for example:

   (a) curl to stretch,
   (b) stretch to curl,
   (c) stretch to stretch,
   (d) curl to curl.

This can be done on the spot, about the spot or about the room.

3. Use the mats as in (1) but vary the means of weight transference used for getting up to, over, and away from the mat in the following ways:

   (a) Use the same transference of weight for getting up to and away from the mat, and a different one to get over it.

   (b) Use a different transference of weight in each case to get up to, over, and away from the mat.

   (c) Use the same transference of weight in each case to get up to, over, and away from the mat.

LESSON FOURTEEN

1. Get over mat in a variety of ways using different directions and levels.

2. Now think about putting body into curl and stretch shapes as you do this.

3. Resume work of previous lesson, *i.e.* working for a continuous sequence of movement to get up to, over, and away from the mat using a variety of weight transferences.

4. Fix one sequence and practise it. Thus we have experience in a sequence of movement of moving in as many different ways as possible and also in one way only, and of having continual practice in that one way.

LESSON FIFTEEN

1. Get over the form or bench on to the mat without touching the form with your body, using different directions and levels, and with a variety of body shape.

2. In a space on the floor find different ways of putting legs:

   (*a*) close to one another and close to the rest of the body,
   (*b*) close to one another and away from the rest of the body,
   (*c*) far away from one another and the rest of the body,
   (*d*) away from one another and close to the rest of the body,
   (*e*) with one leg close to and one leg away from the rest of the body.

3. Get over the form on to the mat in different ways with legs in the above positions. Ways of using the apparatus can be as follows:

   (*a*) taking weight on hands on form, using one or both hands (either together or one after the other),
   (*b*) taking weight on hands on mat,
   (*c*) taking weight with one hand on the form and one hand on the mat,
   (*d*) taking weight on feet on the form, using either one or both feet (together or one after the other).

4. Fix one way and practise it. A sequence of movement can then be established as before in getting up to, over, and away from the apparatus.

LESSON SIXTEEN

1. Move about the room in different ways with legs close together and with legs apart, using different directions and different levels.

2. On the spot find different ways of sitting, standing and lying with legs together and with legs apart.

3. Using forms and mats (Fig. 3) move over the form on to the mat with legs together and with legs apart.

Again establish a continuous sequence of movement to get up to, over, and away from the form and to get along or over the mat to finish.

4. Fix one way and practise it.

Apparatus plan

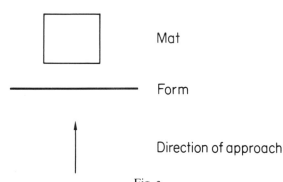

Fig. 3.

LESSON SEVENTEEN

1. Using the apparatus (Fig. 4) in any way you like, get up to form with legs close to one another, use the form with legs away from one another, and use the mat with legs close to one another.

2. Again using apparatus in your own way, get up to form with legs away from one another, use the form with legs close to one another, and use the mat with legs away from one another.

Apparatus plan

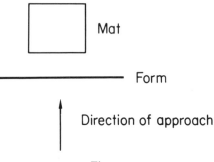

Fig. 4.

If necessary one way of using part of the apparatus can be set, *e.g.* take your weight on hands when using the form.

3. Find different ways of getting over the form by jumping, for example:

   (*a*) jump over without touching it,
   (*b*) jump on—jump off,
   (*c*) jump over using one or two feet on the form to do so.

Here we have the introduction of a vaulting technique, *i.e.* to jump over the form we have a take-off, followed by flight in the air, followed by a landing on the mat. The children should be encouraged to make different body shapes in the air with legs in different positions when jumping.

4. Now make up a sequence of running and jumping over the form (as above) to land on the mat and continue along the mat with a subsequent transference of weight, *e.g.* forward roll, etc. Thus again we have a continuous sequence of getting up to, over, and away from the apparatus, or a sequence of approaching the apparatus, using it, and moving away from it to finish the sequence. In all these sequences a held or stationary balance may also be included if desired—that is to say, at any point in the sequence the movement may be arrested and weight taken on any part or parts of the body and held there in a position of balance before continuing the sequence.

PARTNER, GROUP AND SMALL APPARATUS WORK
(Lessons One to Three)

LESSON ONE: Partner work—making bridges

1. One partner makes a bridge with his body—the other partner goes under and over this bridge. Find a variety of ways to make bridges and to get under and over them. Work for continuity of movement in dealing with the bridge and special care should be given to shape and form whether one is acting as the bridge or one is coping with it.

2. One partner goes under or over the bridge and then turns into the bridge himself for the other partner to follow suit, repeating this arrangement and movement sequence.

This work can be coped with in different ways, for example:

   (*a*) the "bridge" can alter shape and position in order to facilitate movement of partner and to aid continuity;
   (*b*) you can start on one side of the "bridge" and finish on the other side;
   (*c*) you can start on one side of the "bridge," go to the other side, and then back to your original starting position;

(*d*) this can be done with or without actually holding on to the "bridge;"

(*e*) this can be done with or without the "bridge" holding you in some way to facilitate your movement.

LESSON TWO: Group work

1. Work in groups of four with one acting as a body, two as supporters and one as the performer. The task is to lift the performer over the body in a variety of ways, for example:

(*a*) by lifting the performer completely over the body,

(*b*) by lifting the performer partly over the body and then letting them go,

(*c*) by lifting the performer over the body in stages,

(*d*) by lifting the performer over the body at the beginning or end of the activity.

This can be done from a running take-off or from a preparation to lifting on the spot. It can also be done with or without the performer touching the person acting as the body. It is important to find a variety of positions when acting as the body, for example, a position with the front of the body facing the floor or ceiling, or a position on hands or feet, etc.

LESSON THREE: Small apparatus work

1. Working with a partner, using a hoop, balance the hoop between you. Progress to lifting it up and putting it down between you. Find a variety of ways to do this using different parts of the body to do so.

2. Give the hoop to one another finding a variety of ways to do this and using different parts of the body to give and take the hoop.

3. Working on your own using a ball, find different ways of bouncing the ball using different parts of the body with which to bounce it, for example:

(*a*) hands:

(*i*) back of hand,
(*ii*) palm of hand,
(*iii*) heel of hand,
(*iv*) fingers,
(*v*) side of hand,

(*b*) feet,
(*c*) elbow,
(*d*) head, etc.

4. Bounce the ball high, low, near to and far away from your body, from near to far and vice versa.

5. Find out how many different ways you can bounce the ball in relationship to your body, for example:

(*a*) under a leg,
(*b*) round the back of your body,
(*c*) between your legs,
(*d*) in front of your body.

6. Now progress to working with a partner throwing and catching or bouncing the ball between you, using the previous experimental work.

MOVEMENT FACTORS OR EFFORT ACTIONS IN EDUCATIONAL GYMNASTICS

This work is concerned with the basic action of a vault, *i.e.* take-off, flight and landing. It concerns the impact action of a vault and the impulse action of a recovery or landing, and an agility. It is necessary to be aware of the movement effort actions needed to cope with this work, which are pushing, pulling, swinging or rocking, or a combination of these leading into taking or transference of weight. In order to achieve effort actions a preparation is required, whether it be a travelling one, such as a run (in order to vault), or a preparation on the spot, for example, a rebound (for agilities or low apparatus work). Speed, whether quick or sustained, is also required, also tension, control or grip throughout the whole of the effort action, for on landing the body weight should be controlled by the performer, not vice versa. The effort action made is either from the floor or from the apparatus into the space or the air and ends in recovery, landing or subsequent impulse, flight, and glide (if there is a further transference of weight) on the floor or apparatus.

LESSON ONE: The effort action of pushing on the floor

In weight control we can push against, from, or from and on to various body parts or pieces of apparatus, or floor, etc.

1. Find different ways of pushing your weight from hands to feet and back again.

2. Find ways of pushing with hands against the floor, and of pushing from the floor with feet. Experiment with the number of hands or feet you can use to do this.

3. Find ways of pushing your weight on to different parts of the body and by pushing against the floor to balance there in a held stationary position. Use broad and narrow bases to balance on, thinking about how and where and on what parts of the body the body weight is

distributed. Also think about maintaining a good body shape whilst in position of balance.

4. Find ways of transferring your weight by pushing the body weight from different parts of the body on to other parts.

5. Make up a sequence of stationary and continuous balance, *i.e.* taking and transference of weight. Work for continuity of movement and body shape and a good controlled effort action of pushing body weight where you want to take it or transfer it.

LESSON TWO: The effort action of pushing on apparatus

1. Find different ways of pushing from feet to transfer weight from forms on to the floor, and from the floor on to forms. Use different combinations of feet, *e.g.* two to two, one to two, two to one, one to one, etc.

2. On the forms find different ways of pushing weight from hands and/or feet in order to get on and off the form or in order to get over it, *e.g.* crouch jump or extension jump on and off or over the form.

Thus in this work we have the effort action of pushing:

(*a*) from the floor,
(*b*) from the apparatus,
(*c*) from the apparatus on to the floor in order to get on, off or over apparatus for purposes of weight transference.

In addition we have the effort action of pushing:

(*i*) against the floor, *e.g.* handstand (to take weight);
(*ii*) against the apparatus, *e.g.* handstand (to get off), crouch jump, leap-frog, etc.;
(*iii*) weight from feet onto hands and vice versa on the floor and on the apparatus, *e.g.* handstand, cartwheel, crouch jump;
(*iv*) weight from feet and hands to get off apparatus, e.g. crouch jump in order to get on, off or over apparatus for purposes of weight taking as well as transference.

The effort action of pushing in gymnastics is used in a variety of ways and for several purposes, for example:

1. to push weight from or off the apparatus or the floor mainly for an action or vault;
2. to push against the floor and apparatus mainly to take weight for a stationary balance;
3. to push weight on to apparatus and floor and on to different body parts mainly to transfer weight for continuous balance.

LESSON THREE: Teaching the effort action of pushing by a basic movement approach

The effort action of pushing, which is required for purposes of take-off, flight and landing, is the basis of all vaults whether quick or sustained.

1. On the spot, on the floor, jump for me:

  (*a*) How do we get off the floor?—By pushing.
  (*b*) What helps us to get high in the air?—Lifting our head up, throwing our arms up.
  (*c*) What keeps us in the air?—Tension, grip, position of stretch.
  (*d*) How do we land?—Relax, and then be ready to continue moving if necessary.

2. Run and jump for me:

  (*a*) What helps us to get our body further away from the ground? —Speed, adding a run to our take-off push.
  (*b*) What kind of a run do we need?—Quick, long or short.
  (*c*) When do we jump?—When we see a space if jumping from the floor into the air, or before we get to the particular piece of apparatus if using apparatus.
  (*d*) When do we stop running and start taking off?—When we are almost up to the apparatus, or when we have chosen a space on the floor.
  (*e*) What do we do in between running and taking off?—Bring feet together if a double take-off is required.

Thus there is a slight pause when the run must lead or flow into the take-off, *i.e.* the actual push or moment of take-off. Children must not sink into the floor between running and taking-off or go on running into the actual take-off. If they do there is no push at all or a great "tiger bound" when all impetus is lost.

  (*f*) What direction are we pushing in?—Upwards or outwards.
  (*g*) Where is the main impetus?—The run or the take off. When do we need to accelerate in speed?—When the run is about to become or lead into the take-off.

3. Put the above work on to forms—running and jumping on to and then off forms.

  (*a*) How many pushes have we?—Two, *i.e.* one to take us from the floor on to the form and one to take us from the form on to the floor.
  (*b*) How do we take off from the floor and from the form?— Single or double take-off.

4. Go on to explore the different ways of taking off and landing on different combinations of feet on both floor and apparatus, for example:

  (*a*) from two to two feet,
  (*b*) from one foot to two feet,
  (*c*) from two feet to one foot,
  (*d*) from one foot to one foot (same or different foot).

Emphasise that whilst doing this we can make different shapes with the body and that the shape of the body whilst in flight is very important.

5. Using apparatus find ways of using the different combinations of feet to take off.

(*a*) from the floor on to a form,
(*b*) from the floor on to double forms, or a low box, etc.
(*c*) from the beating board,
(*d*) from forms inclined on bars,
(*e*) from big apparatus with a form or beating board in front of it—
so we go from one piece of apparatus to another.

6. Using apparatus find different ways of taking weight on to hands and then feet to get on to and then off apparatus. This can be done:

(*a*) on single forms,
(*b*) on double forms,
(*c*) on a low box,
(*d*) on big apparatus with forms or beating boards.

Thus we get a transference of weight from hands to feet to get on and then back again to get off apparatus.

7. Using the ropes, either single or double or knotted together, find ways of taking off from the floor to lead into flight on to the ropes. How do we do this? We do this:

(*a*) by taking a run and jumping on to a stationary rope,
(*b*) by running with the rope, moving hands up the rope as you travel (either both together or hand over hand).

Consider and think about the following:

(*i*) What kind of a take-off or push do we use to get from the floor on to the rope?—single or double.

(*ii*) Is it a complete take-off which takes us straight from the floor to stay on the rope in flight, or do we come down to the floor again to run in order to get another push or take-off?

(*iii*) What do we do with our body on the rope? What shape do we make? Where do we put our hands and feet on the rope? Which part of our body takes our weight on the rope?

(*iv*) How do we get off?—by jumping off forwards or backwards either by letting go of the rope or retaining hold of it, or by some other means of transferring our weight off the rope, *e.g.* somersault whilst on rope and then land onto feet on the floor.

(*v*) How many feet do we land on? On to what part or parts of our body do we transfer our weight whilst in flight on the rope or in landing on the floor?

A very important point concerned with all of this work is: at what stage in the school do we do it? There is a good argument for doing this in the first or second year of the senior school or as early as possible, otherwise girls may be too heavy (early maturity), or too timid, and this basic work is needed before children can successfully cope with big apparatus. This is basic work to illustrate how to get flight, how to take off—the use of the effort action of pushing. It is a basis for experimentation and the children should be encouraged to think about this basic work and its application whichever piece of apparatus they use when a push or take-off is required. Children tend to climb and crawl and flop from the floor on to apparatus and to flop and fall from apparatus on to the floor. The above work should eliminate this tendency.

LESSON FOUR: The effort action of swinging

The effort actions of swinging, pulling and pushing and the combination of all three must be mastered in order to achieve successful results on apparatus. The take-off, flight and landing stages must be stressed.

1. On the spot, on the floor, find various ways of swinging legs, taking weight on different parts of the body in order to get the rest of the body in the air, *e.g.* handstand to take weight on the hands and swing the legs into space.

2. Find ways of travelling by swinging the legs into space, *e.g.* cartwheel, handstand into crab, jumps taking weight on hands with legs in different directions, jumps with weight on feet slashing legs through space in different directions. This is *instantaneous* travelling.

3. Find ways of travelling with a preparation, for example:

   (*a*) swing, swing and arrive, *e.g.* standing broad jump;

   (*b*) running into a swing, *e.g.* run into a cartwheel, etc.;

   (*c*) running into a take-off and swing, *e.g.* running dive into forward roll.

4. Using mats, and forms and mats, find ways of employing this apparatus using the above ideas on floorwork, for example:

   (*a*) take weight on hands and swing the body over the apparatus, *e.g.* cartwheel and preparation to front and fence vault;

   (*b*) jump off and over forms using body swing, *e.g.* high jump scissor kick, western roll action.

It is necessary to point out to the children the action of the legs that is required, and also the role that other parts of the body must play, for example, hands taking weight, feet pushing from the floor, in order to achieve the correct effort action.

5. On the ribstalls find different body positions in which to balance, *e.g.* front, back or side of body to the ribstall. Now swing body away from the ribstall to land on the floor. On this and all apparatus bear in mind that the swing can be either instantaneous or prepared as illustrated in the previous floorwork lessons.

6. On ropes (single or double), taking weight on different parts of the body, find different ways of swinging, *e.g.* reverse hanging, crow's nest, somersaults, long arm swing, etc. The body must swing, not just the rope.

7. Using single and double bars find different ways of travelling in different directions by using body swing, *e.g.* through vault, sheep thro' the gap, fence and front vault.

8. Using saddles fixed on bars find different ways of swinging the body through the saddle (quick and sustained), *e.g.* slow squat, thief, wolf.

Point out to the children that to achieve an effort action of swing two actions are required, firstly, the inclusion and use of further effort actions, *e.g.* pushing and/or pulling for purposes of take-off, and secondly, a body action—that of swing for flight—and that the effort action must be converted into the landing in order to finish the vault or activity.

9. With a partner, or in groups of three, find different ways of swinging a body off the floor using various body holds, for example:

(*a*) upward jump in threes,
(*b*) honey pot in threes,
(*c*) in twos swinging one another holding neck by hands, hands by hands, hands by one hand and one leg, etc.

LESSON FIVE: The effort action of pulling

1. Find various ways of pulling yourself along the floor in different directions, *e.g.* trout up stream, caterpillar walk. What parts of the body are being used in order to do this?

2. Find various ways of pulling a partner along the floor, *e.g.* elbows linked with elbows, back to back positions, etc.

3. Using straight or inclined forms find different ways of pulling yourself along in different directions, taking weight on different parts of the body and using different body parts to push and pull.

4. Find different ways of pulling your body from the floor up on to the ribstalls.

5. Find different ways of pulling your body up on to a rope from different positions, for example:

    (*a*) from lying on the floor,
    (*b*) from a standing upright position,
    (*c*) from a running take-off.

It is necessary to point out to the children the need for either an effort action of pull followed by a recovery movement, or a preparation action leading into a pulling action and subsequent recovery movement, in order to achieve successful body transference from floor to apparatus and vice versa; in other words, the use of instantaneous pull or pull with preparation as in previous work on the floor and in work in other effort actions.

6. Using bars (single and double), find different ways of pulling yourself over, *e.g.* somersault, and movement along, as in the monkey crawl. Use different parts of the body in contact with the apparatus to take or support body weight and body transference.

It should be noted that, in lessons concerned with the effort actions of pushing, swinging, pulling and their combination, although the illustrated lesson plans may seem to some to be too directed, a certain amount of direction or specific guidance is justified in the author's opinion, as long as scope is given for experimentation in addition. The reason for this opinion is that children do not accidentally stumble on the correct effort force required for these actions, and therefore it is perhaps a help to make them *aware* of same.

MOVEMENT SHAPES IN EDUCATIONAL GYMNASTICS

Work on these can be done on the floor and on the apparatus. We have the following categories to consider:
Curl shapes.
Stretch (narrow and wide) shapes.
Shapes which move from curl to stretch.
Shapes which move from stretch to curl.
Shapes which move from stretch to stretch.
Shapes which move from curl to curl.
Shapes where part of the body is curled and part stretched.
Shapes which are either straight or twisted.

When making the above movement shapes children should be made aware of their use and for what reason or purpose we make these shapes. We make them:

(*a*) for control of weight purposes—the taking and transference of weight for purposes of (or to assist in) stationary balance, for locomotion, for flight and on landing or recovery;

(*b*) for aesthetic purposes.

In this and the subsequent chapters dealing with educational gymnastics, the apparatus used is generally that found more commonly in senior schools than in junior and/or primary and infant schools. It is possible, however, to substitute apparatus used in the last-mentioned schools, for example, climbing frames can be substituted for ribstalls and padded trestles or movement tables for forms or boxes, etc. A certain amount or a slight amount of improvisation with regard to the work content may be necessary when so doing.

It will also be noted that examples given of certain work are couched in formal gymnastic language instead of, or in addition to, movement terminology. This is to allow for the understanding of readers trained in different methods of physical education.

Chapter Five

EDUCATIONAL GYMNASTICS: I

THE GYMNASTIC PROBLEM

Sooner or later the student and/or teacher is faced with the problem of the meaning of modern educational gymnastics, and what is their purpose and aim. Educational gymnastics are creative and are concerned with the mastery of movement, with various actions on apparatus, and with the ability to meet certain and various challenges the apparatus may offer. They give opportunity for individual, partner and group work where both creative ideas and a high standard of practical performance are necessary. They are concerned with weight control, body and space awareness, effort actions, locomotion and speed. Children have to have a mastery of movement and a mastery of apparatus in order to cope successfully with educational gymnastics. The aim is to teach the apparatus—its use and scope—not merely a lesson theme. Children cannot bring out and use their ideas effectively unless they can cope with the apparatus—ideas are dependent not only upon the child's mastery of movement but also upon its use of apparatus.

In order to facilitate both there are several needs to be met in teaching this particular branch of physical education. These needs, and the way to meet and cater for them, vary according to the individual class, but from the teaching point of view may generally be classed as follows:

1. The need to set a movement task in order to guide through suggestion.
2. The need to set a framework of apparatus.
3. The need for no set task or apparatus framework, *i.e.* the need for free experiment based on the application of experience of floorwork to the apparatus.

4. The need to coach and improve the ideas and mastery of movement of individual children.

5. The need for the children to realise and recognise the main divisions in educational gymnastics in floorwork and on apparatus which may be classed as follows:

> (*a*) a vault, *e.g.* leap-frog, which is an action complete in itself fighting against time and weight,
>
> (*b*) an agility, *e.g.* cartwheel, which is a continuous action using time and weight,
>
> (*c*) a static balance which is the control of time and weight.

The above movements (*a*)–(*c*) can be separate or isolated, or two or all three can be combined, or one can be converted or lead into others, for a movement sequence on the floor or apparatus.

The ultimate aim behind educational gymnastics should be for the children eventually to build up their own apparatus sequences, to set their own apparatus tasks and to work on both, using their own movement ideas rather than working on a set theme or task. Before this can happen successfully, however, the children must have mastery of a range of movement allied to body awareness in relationship to space (directions and levels), weight (the use and control of it), time (the ability to fight against and indulge in it) and flow (continuous or arrested). In body awareness the stress must not only be on body shape and form, but also on the different parts of the body that can come into contact with or take weight on both the floor and the apparatus.

The crucial problem in teaching educational gymnastics is one of guidance—how much to give, the nature of it, and what form this guidance should take. This problem can be met by selection of teaching method, selection of apparatus and a knowledge and understanding of difficulties that may arise in the work. Upon the question of teaching method a skill must be acquired, and children, as said before, must develop an agility on apparatus to be really happy. This is a strong argument for guidance at least in the initial stages of the work. Guidance can allow for freedom of choice and exploration, whereas if the guidance factor is completely lacking and work is absolutely free all the time, one cannot set up a realistic yardstick by which to measure it. It is important, therefore, that the guidance is suited to the yardstick and vice versa. Remember that if a child solves a movement problem literally it cannot be wrong—so care must be taken as to the manner and way in which movement problems or tasks are posed or set. Confusion in the mind of the teacher results in confusion in his teaching presentation and method which in turn results in confusion in the movement and minds of the children. If a child has solved the problem the teacher cannot justifiably be upset if it did not do so in the way she had in mind—guidance should be given to facilitate the child's powers of creative movement, not those of the teacher. In addition, if no guidance is given at all—there being only exploratory work—there is often no way of assessing a child's capabilities or needs, and this therefore can lead to lack of progression.

If one is to take the children's ideas one must be able to visualise their aim and help them to achieve it and progress further, otherwise one is not extending their movement range and vocabulary. Purely exploratory work will accustom children to the apparatus and satiate their creative need, but it can also exhaust this need and result in vague undisciplined movement. Exceptional classes can, of course, apply their floorwork very happily to apparatus without further guidance, but one must beware of the increased problem of early physical maturity, especially in the case of girls. Also, children still need to be aware of or to be made aware of standards of work, and movement memory training should, after all, be an important part of all their work.

Once the student and/or teacher has, after observation and assessment of the class, decided upon the necessity and amount of guidance needed she must then face the problem of how to give it. Several variations and possibilities can be used as follows:

1. The teacher setting up a movement sequence or apparatus task and guiding the work through suggestion.

2. The teacher setting up a movement sequence or apparatus task and the work being set partly or wholly by the class.

3. The teacher setting up different apparatus groups and the work being set entirely by the class.

4. The class setting up different apparatus groups and working on them entirely alone.

5. The class setting up different apparatus groups and the work, movement sequence or task being set by the teacher.

6. The teacher setting both the apparatus and the work, movement sequence or apparatus task.

Possibilities (1)–(2) can be done with everyone working on the same apparatus and (3)–(6) can be done with everyone working on different apparatus groups, but changing round to give the children comprehensive apparatus experience.

In considering which of the above possibilities or alternatives to choose it is necessary to bear in mind that this depends entirely upon the needs and ability of a particular class, and upon whether educational gymnastics are being introduced into a school, or whether there is a continuation or progression of same. Consideration must also be given as to at what particular stage and with which particular age-group the work is being done. From the author's experience in senior schools it may be said that possibilities (1)–(2) are suitable for first-year work and for girls lacking earlier movement and apparatus experience. Possibilities (3)–(4) are suitable for second-year work and upwards. Possibility (3) is especially suitable for second and third years. Possibility (4) is suitable for capable third and fourth years and should also work extremely well with fifth and sixth years—indeed should be the goal for which they should work provided that they have had sufficient movement experience lower down the school. Possibility (5) can be an interesting challenge to fourth, fifth and sixth years who have apparatus experience. Possibility (6) is good for slow thinkers or very limited performers, or those not used to modern methods. This is the least of all alternatives to be recommended, but can be quite effective when changing over from formal to modern methods.

The amount of direction or guidance can also be increased by fixing either the apparatus, such as the actual height of the beam or bar, or by fixing the action by, for example, telling the children to get through the saddle, and thus *what* to do, or by telling them, for example, to take their weight on their hands, thus *how* to do it. Alternatively, one can fix the body movement or shape, for example, knees kept close to body and/or close to one another as you get through the saddle.

Further suggestions as to the amount of guidance necessary and how to give it are as follows:

1. For first and second years—having fixed the apparatus, allow for experimental work, asking for different ways of coping with it using different directions and levels and making different body shapes.

2. For second years—fix the apparatus only, reminding children of the importance of the application of their movement training to the apparatus. Fix the action and/or body shape if the class appears to be getting creatively exhausted, as may often happen, or if they appear to have difficulty in meeting the challenge of the apparatus.

3. The third and fourth years—fix the apparatus, and if the children are sufficiently capable leave the rest to the class, or do not attempt to set even the apparatus framework if the class has reached a very good standard of work by this stage. If children have acquired an agility and mastery on and off apparatus by the late third or fourth year, they are happy to select their own apparatus, arrange and work on it in complete freedom, and, as has been said previously, this is the ultimate goal for good work in the fifth and sixth forms.

4. For classes who experience a great deal of difficulty in one form or another, fix the apparatus, the action, the way to do it and the body shape, and gradually lead the class to the stage where the children can rely upon their own efforts, creative powers and ability.

In dealing with the question of selection of apparatus it is necessary to compare the procedure adopted in the old or formal way of teaching with that used in present methods. In the formal method we had a lesson theme based or built up on a warming and limbering stage, followed by one of mobilising and strengthening, leading up to the final climax of an activity. The children were given experience of all apparatus—often of several pieces in one lesson. This worked quite happily because the task was directed, but loss of time was bound to take place, and the apparatus still had to be suited to the ability of the class in order to make the lesson at all possible. Added to which, a considerable amount of time had to be spent in giving directions for moving and getting out or putting away apparatus.

In the new, informal or creative method of teaching gymnastics the aim is to build up from simple to compound apparatus using only one or two pieces of apparatus during the whole lesson. This approach is more suited to modern methods as children now have the task of coping not only with the apparatus but also with their bodies in an individual relationship to it, and with their own creative ideas and mental processes of thought rather than with a "computer fed" directed task. A great advantage is that very little teaching and working time is lost. In the formal method when children were on more compound or complicated apparatus, only those with natural ability would seem to be coping in a successful way—but an inexperienced teacher could, and often did, put this down to the children's lack of experience, or lack of progression, or lack of courage, without realising that all these aforementioned qualities, which are so vital to the success of a good lesson, stem from good teaching which gives opportunity for the children to acquire and develop them, rather than from mere persistent use of the apparatus itself. The only way to see this clearly is to put first-year children in a secondary school on compound and complicated apparatus, and the folly of this will soon be apparent. Children can, after all, absorb only so much at a time, and if they are later to achieve the ultimate and build up their own apparatus arrangements they must be fully conversant with the scope of the apparatus and how to move it. If they are familiar with each piece and the drill thereof they can cope quite happily. If put on to big apparatus straight away they tend to concentrate on this and ignore the simple pieces of apparatus like mats, for example. Mats are now a piece of working apparatus, not merely "landing cushions."

If experience of apparatus is built up gradually, no loss of time is spent in giving out detailed instructions for its transportation every lesson—the class at the beginning of the next lesson can start getting out and working on apparatus without waiting for the whole class to assemble and then be given directions. With regard to the manipulation of the travelling upright and bars or the adjustment in height of the horse or buck, it is necessary for the teacher to give specific instructions as to the manner in which this is carried out— one would not expect a class to experiment and find out because of the obvious danger of accident or damage to apparatus. This instruction can now, however, be given as a composite part of the lesson and can be built up as the use and experience of apparatus is built up, side by side and in conjunction with one another. Some teachers may still feel, however, that it is preferable to devote a lesson solely to apparatus manipulation as an alternative solution, but if this is done it is best, in the author's opinion, for it to take the form of a sitting and watching lesson with the children clothed, rather than submit a class to the frustration of changing into physical education clothing for work and then spending the entire lesson observing and freezing at the same time because of inadequate clothing.

In an apparatus lesson the aim of the class should be to use apparatus as much as possible, but effectively and to good purpose. It is also a good idea if children are encouraged from the beginning to think about planning out the spacing of their own apparatus with regard to the class at work without always being instructed by the teacher exactly whereabouts in the room to put each or their own particular piece.

Experience of all the different pieces of apparatus must definitely be given, but this should be done by building up different and varied heights of apparatus, building up movement sequences on it and adding to it as the children become familiar with each separate piece. One must, of course, ensure that progression is made and experience of all apparatus (at low heights) is gained before children become overweight, and lack of enthusiasm or fear of the apparatus has set in. As the emphasis is on apparatus and skill in dealing with it, according to the needs of the class, the lessons can be taken with all children working on the same piece of apparatus, which, if necessary, can be graded according to the height and ability of the performer, and/or with children working on different pieces of apparatus of a different nature, each piece of apparatus presenting a varying degree of difficulty. Here it may be necessary to allocate particular pieces of apparatus according to the abilities of the class, or it may be possible for all children to cope successfully with each piece; or a transition from the first method of working to the second method can be achieved.

One of the main problems in the teaching of educational gymnastics is the difficult question of children posing on apparatus. Gymnastics may well become acrobatic dance which in itself may not be a bad thing, but different apparatus is needed at times for it to become a purposeful activity. If one is to include and allow different variations of educational gymnastics the apparatus must be suited to the needs of the work as well as the work being suited to the apparatus. In addition to retaining the old apparatus, could we not add to it and improve upon its original design by, for example, having three instead of two parallel bars or beams with a fixed and travelling upright, and have wider and padded forms or benches, plus new apparatus designs such as body-bouncing harness, etc.? Then, by the very nature of the apparatus itself as well as by the nature of the movement, children could become aware of the three main categories into which educational gymnastics can be divided. These are as follows:

1. A vault, in which there are three interlocking movements or actions of take-off, flight whilst in balance, and landing. Here the emphasis is on effort action with weight control (transference of weight). We have mostly impact movements —movements fighting against time with direct and indirect pathways and symmetrical and asymmetrical body shapes.

2. An agility on apparatus. Here the emphasis is on body awareness with relation to effort action. We have mostly movements indulging in weight or using weight (transference of weight) with direct and indirect pathways, and symmetrical and asymmetrical body shapes.

3. Acrobatic or dance-like movements on apparatus which are concerned with positions mainly of stationary or held balance. Here the emphasis is on shape and form with rela-

tionship to space awareness and weight control (taking of weight) and is often condemned as being "ornamental" or "movement performed for movement's sake," when it is often work which contains very good body agility and *poise*, not pose.

Hence, in all work concerned with apparatus, the movement must be suited to the particular apparatus and vice versa. To differentiate between these three categories of movement on apparatus, the nature of the apparatus and/or the guidance given on it will produce the type of movement required coupled with floorwork experience. This again leads to another of the main problems in the teaching of educational gymnastics—namely, that of the application of floorwork done in basic movement lessons or in gymnastics lessons to the apparatus work. With some classes this is automatic and instantaneous but with others more help and guidance with this particular task is necessary in order to bridge the gap successfully.

CREATIVE IDEAS IN EDUCATIONAL GYMNASTICS

These are obtained by using the following:

1. Different directions in which to work.
2. Different parts of the body on which to arrive, be, or take weight on the apparatus, or on which to leave it. In other words, by using different parts of the body for weight control (taking and transference) purposes.
3. Different actions on the apparatus—to get over, or on and off, or along, or through or under and various combinations of these.
4. Different effort actions—by using swing or rock, or push or pull or various combinations of these.
5. Different body shapes—by making stretch (narrow and wide) or curl shapes and various combinations of these.
6. Different levels—by getting the body away from or close to the apparatus and various combinations of these.
7. Different speeds at which to move—by moving quickly or with sustainment, and the combination of both.

In other words, ideas are created and performed by thinking in terms of where we go in space, with what part or parts of our body, and how in terms of speed and for how long in terms of flow.

How is this carried out?

We can get over, under, through, across, along, on, off and around apparatus, and in addition use a combination of these when working on apparatus. With regard to the simple action of take-off preparatory to flight and landing, we can take-off over, on to, off, through, across or along apparatus, and it is through experience of locomotion on the floor and apparatus that children can acquire the skill of vaulting—that is, the need and effective execution of a take-off, flight and landing. If children are not made aware of and coached in these principles they may always rely upon climbing, scrambling or flopping off the apparatus. This is a good case for movement training on the floor where these basic needs for coping with apparatus can be acquired.

Children need to be aware of *arrival on apparatus*; that is, to be aware of what parts of the body are put on the apparatus (hands, feet, etc.), of *exactly* which part of the apparatus the body is placed on, and of *exactly* the spot where they are going to alight. If the children are going to climb, the same thing applies as equally as it does in vaulting or jumping. Thus on apparatus it is necessary to stress the action above all, coupled with body awareness and speed, to produce different ideas and ways of coping with it. Ideas must be converted into locomotion or action and carried out using the body and its parts effectively with the correct speed required.

The subject of locomotion brings us to the question of the use of the spring-board or beating board. In the author's opinion children should be taught, after a certain amount of experimentation, how to use this piece of apparatus, for in order to get the maximum and most efficient use from it the skill of using it must be acquired. A useful way is to combine it with the agility mattress, so we get a sequence of run into beat or take-off (single or double), into flight (upward or outward) into landing, with subsequent transference of weight along the mattress. Although the actual skill has been directly taught, after the basis of experimentation, the above sequence gives plenty of scope for experimentation within the taught or acquired skill.

The question of speed is another important factor concerned with locomotion. This, in the author's opinion, should be left to the child. It is difficult for the teacher and often confusing to the child if the teacher tries to assess the speed or amount of preparation required when it is the child's idea, and the teacher cannot be aware of what the child has in mind until she has actually seen it or seen the child struggling to carry it out. Suggestions after this stage are often helpful, but the main emphasis should be on giving the child experience of moving at different speeds in floorwork and in basic movement training. The important point is that if a child means to be quick, it is quick. Thought should also be given to the use of the word "sustained" or "smooth" instead of "slow." The word "slow" in a gymnasium often gives a wrong impression to children and can result in jerky unco-ordinated movements.

To sum up, therefore, on apparatus we work for continuity of approach—how to get on—the actual movement on apparatus—what to do there, and the finish—what to do to get off or how to get off, or how to bring the movement to a close. This is the secret of locomotion on apparatus, and in order to make it completely successful precision of take-off, arrival and landing is essential. To achieve this children must be encouraged to work out for themselves the effort action required, the distance of the run, etc., and the speed at which work is performed. This should not prove too difficult a task if experience of such has been provided in basic movement lessons (*see* Chapter IV: Movement factors or effort actions in educational gymnastics).

To assist in acquiring the skill of vaulting there are several basic preparations for this:

1. Jumps—stressing preparation—take-off, flight and landing; make up different jumps with single and double take-off. Whilst in the

air or in flight find different places to put legs—in front of, behind, to the side of body.

2. Hips above head—how many different ways can you find of getting your hips above your head? Having done this, now use your weight to take or move your body along the ground. Consider how the use of impetus, swing and push can help you. Where can you put your knees down? On either side of, both to one side of, or both to the other side of head? From this one tends to get rolls symmetrical or asymmetrical with legs bent or stretched.

3. Combine (1) and (2) to make a continuous sequence of a jump followed by and leading into a hips above head movement. This can be done on the spot and moving about the room.

4. Arrival on apparatus. This is most important in order to avoid scrambling, flopping, scuttling and clambering. You should aim for a definite and precise transference of weight from floor to apparatus. This may be either partial, complete or immediate and consideration must be given as aforesaid to preparation (on the spot or travelling), speed (quick or sustained), and effort action (pushing, pulling, swinging, etc.).

The following tasks for work on arrival on apparatus may be useful.

(a) Find different ways of arriving on the apparatus using different parts of the body, e.g. hands and feet, hands and seat, hands and tummy, hands and head, hands and knees, feet, hands and legs astride. Find different ways of approaching the apparatus, e.g. from a forwards or sideways direction. To vary this get flight onto the apparatus, arriving with one part of the body and quickly transferring weight on to another part of the body, e.g. from hands to feet, hands to seat, hands to legs astride, etc. Use single and double take-off and work for split second take-off and pounce, and precision of arrival. Having arrived, can you stay and balance on the apparatus?

In all these transference of weight arrivals from floor to apparatus, a certain amount of work in experimentation can be done by the children as to the number of feet from which to take off, the number of body parts to arrive on, the sequence of arrival of these body parts, the shape of the body, and the amount and type of preparation required and effort action needed.

(b) Find different ways or actions of getting over apparatus, without touching it with your body at all, with hands only touching it, with other parts of the body touching it, e.g. hands and head. The work then progresses to arriving, staying on and getting off apparatus by dealing with it in the following ways:

(*i*) Get on—get off.

(*ii*) Get over.

(*iii*) Get part of the body on first followed by the rest of the body, and do the same to get off.

(*iv*) Get part of the body over first followed by the rest.

(*v*) Get on so you land on feet, and get off so you land on feet again.

(*vi*) Get on arriving on feet, transfer weight on to another part of body having arrived and then get off landing on feet.

(*vii*) Get on—balance there in a held position and get off with or without a further transference of weight having arrived on apparatus.

(*viii*) Balance in a position with part of the body on the floor, part on the apparatus. Then transfer the whole of the body on to the apparatus and then get off with a balanced position with part of body on apparatus part of body on floor leading to a complete transference of weight off.

(*ix*) Get on the apparatus, off and then back on again using the same or a different way to do so.

5. Getting off apparatus can be worked in the same manner as arrival on apparatus.

ROPE WORK

The following are specimen lessons on work with both single and double ropes.

LESSON ONE: Creative ideas and body shapes on ropes

1. Find different ways of balancing on the ropes with body in a variety of shapes:

(*a*) with legs away from the body (Plate 1),

(*b*) with legs away from the body and away from one another (Plates 2 and 3),

(*c*) with legs close to the rope,

(*d*) with one leg close to, and one leg away from the rope.

2. Find different ways of getting your body close to and away from the rope, or with the lower part of body away from and the upper part close to the rope (Plate 4).

3. Find different ways of:

(*a*) getting legs above head on the rope,

(*b*) twisting on the rope,

(*c*) curling your body on the rope (Plate 5),

(*d*) stretching your body on the rope.

4. Find different ways of moving your body from one position to another and/or one shape to another on the ropes, *e.g.* from curl to stretch and stretch to curl (Plates 1 and 6).

Plate 1

Plate 2

Plate 3

Plate 4

Plate 5

Plate 6

Plate 7

LESSON TWO: Arrival and balance on ropes

1. Find different ways of getting on to the ropes with *impact, e.g.* step on, jump on, run on, etc.

2. Find different ways of swinging in a balance position thinking about the shape of the body and the position of arms and legs on double ropes or a single rope, or with the greater part of the body more on one rope than on the other. Double ropes may be either knotted or free in this activity.

3. Find different ways of holding on to the rope with different parts of the body in order to stand, kneel, sit, lie on back or tummy, turn upside down, go from one position to another on the ropes.

4. Find different ways of getting off the ropes. This can be done by immediate transference of weight, for example, by jumping off. An alternative way is to get off by partial or delayed transference of weight, that is, to put part of the body down and drag it on the mat until the rope is almost still, and then take the rest of the body off the rope quickly, for example, handstand, headstand or somersault.

5. With or without another person holding the ropes to steady them, find different ways of getting back on to the ropes again having once left them.

6. Find different ways for two people to swing and balance on the ropes at the same time. Find different ways of holding on to the ropes and on to one another with different parts of the body.

LESSON THREE: Work on double ropes

The apparatus for this lesson consists of double ropes (knotted or free) with mats.

1. Find different ways of getting through the ropes on to the mat either with continuous movement or by interrupting the continuity by a held or stationary balance position on the ropes before proceeding on to the mat.

2. Make different body shapes as you do this.

3. Now find different parts of the body to touch the mat first, after or whilst going through the ropes, for example:

    (*a*) hands touching the mat first in a handstand,
    (*b*) head touching the mat first in headstand (Plate 7),
    (*c*) somersault or crouch jump through,
    (*d*) feet touching the mat first to step, jump, swing or somersault through (with hands holding ropes).

Thus in (*a*)–(*d*) we get different parts of the body touching the rope as we go through.

4. Find different directions in which to move to get through the rope and on to the mats.

LESSON FOUR: Getting on, balancing and getting off ropes combined with other apparatus

The apparatus for this lesson consists of:

(*a*) inclined form on double ropes (knotted) and mats,
(*b*) form on the floor leading up to double ropes (knotted) and mats,
(*c*) inclined form on double ropes (knotted) with another knot on the ropes above the form, and mats.

1. Find different ways of getting up and along the form, *e.g.* with hands and feet, or with whole body on the form, or using the floor and the form. Think about the different body shapes you can make whilst doing this.

2. Find different ways of balancing on the ropes making different shapes, using different parts of the body in contact with the rope, using one or both ropes, and with part of the body on the rope, part on the form, and part in the air whilst in position of balance.

3. Find different ways of getting off the ropes, firstly without touching the form, *e.g.* somersault, jump off ropes, and secondly by touching the form, *e.g.* jump off the form, or, with body on form and hands on the mat, handstand, headstand, somersault or crouch jump off.

4. If this work is put into a movement sequence involving other additional apparatus the balance on the ropes can be identified with a balance on that additional piece of apparatus, *e.g.* a saddle on the bar or double bars.

When using ropes in any way the children should be made aware of the different ways of utilising the purpose of ropes in order to cope with work on them. It is, for example, possible to get on to a rope either by running and/or jumping on to a stationary rope, or by taking the rope back with you and travelling forward with it, making the suitable adjustment required in hand-holds. Alternatively, in between getting on to and off the rope or ropes one can run with feet on the floor whilst hands are still holding the rope or ropes in order to gain additional momentum. Possibilities of partner work occur, for a partner can hold the rope or swing the rope to a performer at any required time.

Chapter Six

EDUCATIONAL GYMNASTICS: II

THE WEIGHT FACTOR IN GYMNASTICS

On and off balance

The control of weight is balance, that is, the taking of weight which is static or stationary balance, and the transference of weight which is continuous balance. Static or stationary balance is the taking of weight on the spot, holding and maintaining it there, whilst transference of weight is the moving of weight from one part or parts of the body to a different part or back to the same part or parts of the body. It can be done on the spot or travelling about, and is continuous.

The question of on and off balance and the validity of teaching off balance as a lesson theme occurs in gymnastics. In static or stationary balance, on balance occurs when the centre of gravity is within the points of support, regardless of shape or distribution of weight throughout the body. Off balance is when the centre of gravity moves outside the points of support regardless of shape or distribution of weight throughout the body. In motion, on balance is the transference of weight when the centre of gravity is moving over the *intending* points of support, and off balance is when the centre of gravity is moving outside the *intending* points of support.

The teaching of off balance as a lesson theme is questionable. Rolls should surely be used either as continuity of movement in a movement sequence as a definite transference of weight, or as part of a controlled landing after apparatus work (that is, as part of the apparatus work, for a mat is a piece of apparatus, after all), or as safety training in case of accident. True off balance is flopping, falling and loss of weight control and should surely be avoided in the gymnasium. The term "Let your weight take you" should surely be also avoided—should we not say "Use your weight to take you" and should not the manner of taking be controlled? In weight control we have the use of body grip, tension and control to put or take the body exactly where we want it to go without any "accidents." Prevention is, after all, better than cure—in the gymnasium should not the emphasis be on the acquiring of body control, not losing it? The acquiring of the former will prevent the latter.

An accident happens very quickly and is usually over and done with before the child can do anything about it. Due to the force of gravity there is very little time for the child to "catch its weight" before landing in a heap or flat prone position. Accidents can be disguised by rolling quickly but this does not alter the fact that an accident and loss of weight control has occurred. The value of controlled rolls as safety training has already been mentioned.

The following are specimen lessons on this work.

LESSON ONE: Floorwork

1. Find ways of transferring your weight immediately from spot to spot, *e.g.* jump from feet to feet, using various directions.

2. Find ways of transferring your weight in a delayed manner from spot to spot taking your weight on to various parts of the body and then on to feet, *e.g.* rolling in various directions at different angles or tangents and then coming up on to feet.

3. Combine (1) and (2) together to make a sequence. Single or double take-offs can be used for jumps.

Body grip and a controlled lean into rolls must be coached. The use of different directions, different body parts, symmetrical and asymmetrical shapes, and the use of swing and weight to aid transference of weight must be worked for.

LESSON TWO: Apparatus work

When working on apparatus it is necessary, in addition to the coaching points mentioned previously, to note the importance of *immediate* transference of weight to get on the apparatus, grip and balance there, and the *delayed* transference of weight to get off, and vice versa. Consideration must be given to the possibility of getting on apparatus in one direction and off in another, to the position of legs with regard to their nearness to or distance from the body, the use of hands and body parts to grip and hold on to the apparatus; and most important of all, the question of the intention on floor or apparatus and whether it can be carried out exactly.

(a) beating board and agility mattress,
(b) box at a low height (with or without a beating board on top) and agility mattress,
(c) bar and agility mattress.

Forward somersaults from the beating board and the end of the box. The height at which these are performed, that is, whether in the air or along the agility mattress, must be built up gradually. A run and take-off can precede the somersault. When somersaults on the bar in (c) have been reached the children should be made aware of the "point of drop"—that is, how long hands must hold the bar before letting go for flight through the air. Except for the initial stage of getting on this can then be done without holding the bar with hands at all.

When coaching the children in this work, try to get them to roll or transfer weight in some other way after landing immediately in the initial stages. Make them aware of the necessity for grip and flight in the air and try to get them to come up on to feet at the end of the sequences.

Perhaps, however, this task and the nature of all this work should be referred to as balance and over-balance and not on and off balance. This could be stated in simple terms as action and reaction, for is not what some people refer to as off balance merely the adjustment or re-adjustment of weight in flight or on landing, or of body lean and inclination?

Control of weight allied to floorwork

LESSON ONE: Control of weight by the taking and transference of weight

In this work the position of the legs is important—the position in relation to one another and to the rest of the body. The legs can be in various positions as follows:

(*a*) close to the body and to one another,
(*b*) away from the body and one another,
(*c*) close to the body and away from one another,
(*d*) away from the body and close to one another,
(*e*) one leg close to and one away from the body.

1. Find four positions of balance. These can be achieved by taking weight on different parts of the body to get various positions, with the body on different levels using various directions, and can be done as static balances (taking weight) or as continuous balances (transferring weight), or as a combination of both. Make up a sequence using the four positions of balance chosen.

2. Find different positions of static balance or of taking weight with one leg close to and one leg away from the body. Legs can be near to or far away from one another. Positions in which to do this can be sitting, lying in various ways, standing up, with weight on hands, hands and feet, etc. Choose four after a certain amount of experimentation.

3. Now put a continuous balance or a transference of weight in between the four selected static balances and make up and repeat your sequence. Start in position number one, balance there, move into position number two, balance there, move into position number three, balance there, move into position number four, balance there, move back into position number one, and repeat the whole sequence. Thus each static balance is done in a different spot and continuity of movement transition leading into held balance is achieved.

LESSON TWO: Control of weight in symmetry and asymmetry

On the spot and moving about the room find different ways of jumping in the air followed immediately by different rolls on the floor. Use different directions for the jumps and rolls and symmetrical and asymmetrical shapes for both. Variations are as follows:

(*a*) symmetrical jump, symmetrical roll,
(*b*) asymmetrical jump, asymmetrical roll,
(*c*) symmetrical jump, asymmetrical roll,
(*d*) asymmetrical jump, symmetrical roll.

This particular lesson makes a good warming-up or opening activity to a lesson.

Control of weight by working with a partner

Taking and transference of weight

1. Balance on your partner in various ways of static balance, *e.g.* with whole body on partner, with part of body on partner, and part in the air, with part of body on partner, part in the air and part on the floor.

In order to stay in a held controlled position, consider the question of support needed—is partner merely an inactive body to balance on or do they help as an active support in any way?

2. Now work out ways of getting off your partner by transferring your weight from their body to the floor. The question of the amount of help, if any, given by partner applies again.

3. Make up a sequence with partner taking turns to be the body or support and the performer. Try for continuity in the work of both.

Control of weight by working with apparatus

LESSON ONE: Preparation and resolution or take-off and completion (landing) with regard to taking and transference of weight on apparatus

1. Find different ways of taking and transferring weight on apparatus where the preparation or take-off leads into a position of static or held balance which can then be resolved or completed by a transference of weight back to the original starting position, or can lead to a continuation and subsequent alteration of the original movement in order to get back on to feet again.

Examples are as follows:

(*a*) Take-off into elbow stand on apparatus, with held balance in a position of feet touching head, which can be resolved by transference of weight back down on to feet again, or into transference of weight to go right over and off apparatus with feet going over head.

(*b*) Take-off into held balance in a position of reverse hanging, with hands holding on to the pommels of the horse, which can resolve by transference of weight back down on to the feet again, or into transference of weight to go right over and off apparatus with feet going over head.

In (*a*) and (*b*) the take-off can be single or double and the preparation or transference of weight from floor to apparatus, or on apparatus into actual position of held balance, can be done either up through crouch position, or by a swing up into position.

(*c*) Take-off into held balance in a position of handstand on the pommels of the horse, which can be resolved back down on to feet, or go right over and off apparatus in a walk over transference of weight.

(*d*) Take-off into held balance in a position of handstand on the box, with body sideways to it, with one hand on the floor and one hand holding on to the box at the far side in order to prop weight on that shoulder nearest to the box. This can be resolved by going back down again on to feet, or by continuing over into a forward roll on to box.

The above examples are mainly concerned with transference of weight from feet to hands and back on to feet again, either directly, or by bringing in other parts of the body for weight transference purposes.

LESSON TWO: Preparatory floor work for lesson one

1. Find different ways of getting feet (one or two) close to head in various positions, *e.g.* sitting, standing, kneeling, lying on back, side, or tummy, with hands and feet on the floor, with weight on hands and by getting off the floor.

2. Make up a sequence of several selected positions thinking how you get from one position to another.

3. Now lead into a transference of weight which brings you up on to feet every time in moving from one position to another.

LESSON THREE: Work on ribstalls or wall-bars

1. Find ways of transferring weight from floor on to the ribstalls, balancing there in a held position and then transferring weight back on to the floor again.

In doing this several possibilities and variations are apparent. One must consider the following questions with regard to positions of held balance:

(*a*) How much of the body is on the floor and how much on the ribstall? Is the greater part of body on ribstall or floor? For example, the whole body can be on the ribstall, as in reverse hanging, or part of the body can be on the ribstall and part on the floor, as in the handstand.

(*b*) What parts of body are on the floor and what parts on the ribstall? For example, hands can be on the floor and feet on the ribstall as in the handstand, or feet can be on the floor and hands on the ribstall as in backward crab or back bend position.

(*c*) If the whole of the body is on the ribstall, what part of body is close to it and what part away from it? For example, the back, front or side of body can be close to or away from the ribstall.

(*d*) Is part of the body in the held position of balance in the air as well as on the ribstall? If so, what part or parts and where are they with regard to the rest of the body—near or far?

(*e*) What is the shape of the body in the held position of balance? For example, it can be in a stretch or a curl, or a combination of these two positions. It can be a straight or a twisted balance.

LESSON FOUR: Work on bars or beams (single and double)

1. Find ways of transferring your weight from the floor on to the bar, balancing in a held position and then transferring weight back on to the floor again. Find ways of balancing in the held position with whole body on the bar, with part of the body on the bar and part in the air, or with part on the bar and part on the floor, or with part on the floor, part on the bar and part in the air.

2. Now experiment with balancing on both sides of the bar—the side you get on and the side you reach after getting over.

3. Now experiment with balancing with your body on both sides of the bar—part of it on one side, part on the other.

Control of weight combining floor and apparatus work

LESSON ONE: Floor work

1. The teacher takes a directed activity, for example, leap-frog into forward roll into backward roll for a movement sequence, and coaches the children in this work, stressing continuity of movement.

2. Class now make up a movement sequence of their own involving three ways of transferring weight, working for continuity of movement and a change of speed. This can be done with or without human bodies as obstacles, or apparatus or supports.

LESSON TWO: Apparatus work

The apparatus for this lesson consists of forms and mats.

1. Jumping off forms with a transference of weight from two feet to two feet and/or one foot to two feet. The teacher sets a particular shape, *e.g.* a "long narrow pin stretch" in flight and the children then select their own. The teacher must coach the children in flight and landing. A good landing is important in order to lead into a second transference of weight along the mat. This second transference of weight is experimental but must be combined with the jump for continuity of movement.

2. The class now find ways of taking weight on hands to get over the forms on to the mats and then continue along the mats in a second transference of weight as before.

3. The class now find ways of getting on to and off the forms taking weight on hands and continue as before.

In this lesson the transference of weight from floor to the apparatus, and from one piece of apparatus to another must be stressed, also the transference of weight from one part of the body to another part or parts of it, for example, from feet to hands to feet, to get over the form, and from hands to feet to get on, and from hands to feet to get off again.

LESSON THREE: Further apparatus work

The apparatus for the first part of this lesson consists of:

(*a*) Double ropes (knotted or loose) with a mat or agility mattress in the middle of them. Supports may be used to hold the ropes and assist in the work if required.

(*b*) Box (with or without beating board) and mats on any or all sides.

(*c*) Horse (with or without pommels) and mats on any or all sides.

(*d*) Two inclined forms on ribstalls with a mat in the middle or on any or all sides.

1. Find different ways of transferring weight on apparatus and from one piece of apparatus to another in your sequence of movement.

2. Now include a balance in a held position at some point in your sequence and on some piece of your apparatus. The balance in a held position can be at the beginning, in the middle or at the end of the sequence, and can be on the floor or on the apparatus or on both.

The apparatus for the rest of this lesson consists of:

(*a*) forms and mats,
(*b*) forms, mats and ribstalls as set out in Fig. 5.

3. Find different ways of transferring weight on apparatus and from one piece of apparatus to another in your sequence of movement.

CONTROL OF WEIGHT WITH REGARD TO APPARATUS SEQUENCES AND APPARATUS TASKS

Control of weight—that is, the taking of and transferring of weight—can be done either on apparatus sequences or on apparatus arrangements or tasks. It is essential that in these activities the children should be encouraged to make repeated use of all, or the main, or one single piece or pieces of apparatus. This is achieved by encouraging them to get off a particular piece of apparatus and then straight back on to it again, either severing contact completely with the apparatus or by retaining contact with it with some part or parts of the body as this is done. The children should also be encouraged to use the apparatus from different angles of approach, and different directions in getting on, off and back on to apparatus. Different actions should be used when dealing with the apparatus. It is possible to vault over it by taking the body over in an immediate or complete transference of weight. As

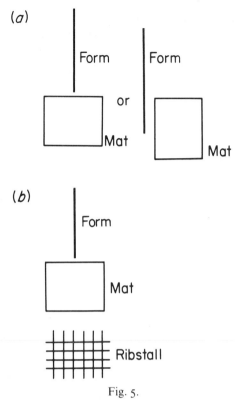

Fig. 5.

an alternative, agilities can be employed to take the body over in a delayed or partial transference of weight. A combination of both will give differences of speed.

Apparatus sequences

In the case of an apparatus sequence, not only do we get continuity of movement but the combination of mobilising and strengthening activities, the combination of floor and apparatus work, and in addition, economy on time lost in getting out apparatus. In an apparatus sequence the teacher can set either the apparatus or the movement task to be performed on it, or both, or these may be set by the class. It is necessary, however, to build up and add to the child's range and apparatus experience if movement sequences are to be used. This can be achieved either by adding a new piece of apparatus to the sequence which also includes familiar apparatus, or by working on a particular piece of apparatus before including it in an apparatus sequence. In the following apparatus sequences the apparatus is given, followed by the movement task and where necessary diagrams are shown.

1. *Apparatus:* form and mat.
   1. Move along the form on to the mat in different ways.
   2. Now think about doing this using different directions and levels and body shapes.
   3. In a space on the floor practise your body shapes to be used.
   4. Select one way and practise this aiming to achieve as high a standard of performance that is possible. Practise the body shapes to be used on the floor or ribstalls whilst awaiting a turn on the apparatus sequence.

2. *Apparatus:* form and mat.
   1. Using different directions, levels and body shapes, find different ways of moving along the form, going from side to side of it without touching the form at all; move away from the form on to the mat to finish the sequence.
   2. Same as in (1) but take your weight on your hands as you move from side to side of the form and then on to the mat.
   3. Do the same as before but this time with some part or parts of your body in contact with the form, *e.g.* weight on hands.
   4. Move along the form keeping on it the whole time and then transfer weight on to the mat.

3. *Apparatus:* form and mat up to ribstall.
   1. Find different ways of going along the form, on to the mat, on to the ribstall and balance there. Moving on to the ribstall into position of balance can be done either by moving straight away into a balance hanging position, *e.g.* reverse hanging, or by climbing on to the ribstall first and then moving into a balance position.

4. *Apparatus:* bar on No. 1 and mat.
   1. Get over the bar on to the mat.
   2. Get over the bar so that hands or feet touch the mat first.
   3. Get over the bar with your body going from curl to stretch position. Curl the body round the bar as you get over, and stretch it as you get off.
   4. Turn the bar over. Now get on, balance there and get off stretching body as you do so.
   5. Get over the bar with as much of your body touching it as possible. Finish on the mat with the body in a curled position.

5. *Apparatus*; inclined form on bar and mat.
  1. Directed activity of "storming" working for elevation, single take-off, flight and relaxation in landing. In other words, run and jump off form.
  2. As before, but experiment with the different body shapes you can make whilst in flight, *e.g.* narrow pin stretch, etc.
  3. Select one particular body shape and practise it on the floor and in the air.

6. *Apparatus:* inclined form on bar and mat.
  1. Find different ways of stretching the body, firstly on the floor and then in the air.
  2. Find different ways of using the apparatus, stretching the body on the apparatus and in the air.
  3. Select one way and practise it. Here again the body shape can be practised on the floor and ribstalls whilst waiting for a turn on the apparatus.

7. *Apparatus:* bar on No. 4 or 5, inclined form and mat.
  1. Free choice of sequence of movement using the apparatus.
  2. Use the apparatus so that hands/feet touch the mat first.
  3. Use the apparatus so that body goes from curl to stretch and vice versa whilst so doing.
  4. Use the apparatus, getting the body as far away from it as possible whilst so doing.

8. *Apparatus:* bar on No. 2 or 3, saddle on bar and mat.
  1. Get through the saddle on to the mat.
  2. Get through with hands/feet touching the mat first.
  3. Get through with body going from curl to stretch as you do so.
  4. Get on to the saddle, balance there and get off stretching body as you do so.
  5. Get through taking weight on hands with legs close to/away from the rest of the body.
  6. Get through with part of the body inside and part of it outside the saddle.

9. *Apparatus*; form inclined on bar No. 1, saddle on bar No. 5 and mat (Fig. 6).
  1. Free choice of movement sequence using the apparatus.
  2. Specify ways of using the saddle, *e.g.* getting through with hands/feet touching the mat first, get on to the saddle and then off, get through taking weight on hands with legs in different positions, etc.
  3. Specify different ways of using the form.

10. *Apparatus:* form inclined on bar No. 1, saddle on bar No. 5, straight form after bar, and mat (Fig. 7).
  1. Get up the inclined form, through the saddle, on to the straight form and on to the mat.

Apparatus sequence

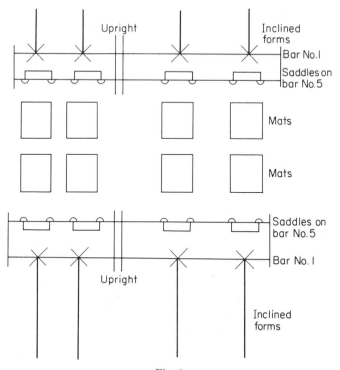

Fig. 6.

2. Do the whole sequence taking weight on hands with legs away from or close to the rest of the body.

3. Get on to the straight form and the mat with hands/feet touching the apparatus first.

4. Do the whole sequence with body stretching/curling all the way.

5. Free choice of sequence but include a held balance on the saddle and on the end of the form (either the inclined and/or straight one).

6. Do the whole sequence with the body as close to the forms as possible and as far away from the saddle as possible.

11. *Apparatus:* straight form up to bar, bar on No. 5, saddle on bar, straight form after bar, mat, bar on No. 5 and mat (Fig. 8).

1. Get up form, through saddle, on to form, along and on to mat, along the floor and over the bar on to mat.

2. Do the whole sequence taking your weight on hands up to the first bar with legs away from or close to body. Get over the bar with legs away from or close to body.

Apparatus sequence

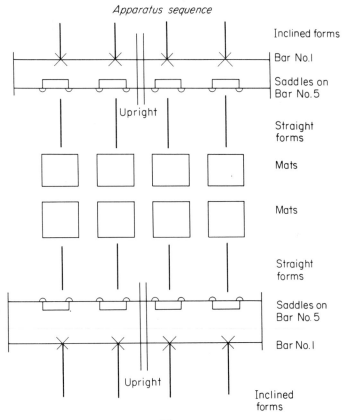

Fig. 7.

3. Get on to the form and mat and along the floor with hands or feet touching the apparatus first.

4. Do the whole sequence with body stretching or curling all the time.

12. *Apparatus:* double bars on Nos. 1 and 11, inclined form on the bottom bar, mat.

1. Using both bars where necessary, move over the top bar and on to the ground alternately. Get off at the end of the sequence with one hand on the top bar and one hand on the bottom one. The sequence can be done stretching legs as far away from the body as possible at some point.

2. Move along the apparatus sequence using the bars and the ground alternately—not necessarily going over the top bar—then get through the double bars on to the mat to finish the sequence.

Apparatus sequence

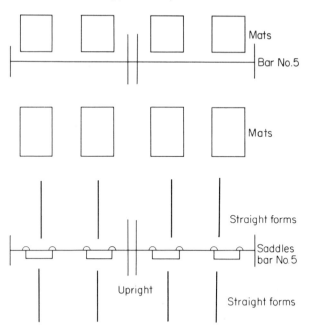

Fig. 8.

3. Work along the sequence with a body curl to get over the top bar and a body stretch to get along between both bars. Choose your own method of getting off to finish the sequence.

13. *Apparatus:* double bars on Nos. 4 and 13, inclined form on bottom bar and mat.
    1. Free experimental choice to work through the sequence.
    2. Work through the sequence with hands or feet touching the mat first.
    3. Work through the sequence with or without using the bottom bar to get on to the mat.
    4. Work through the sequence getting on to the mat with one hand on the top bar and one hand on the bottom bar.
    5. Work through the sequence with legs close to or away from the body.
    6. Work through the sequence with the body in a variety of shapes, *e.g.* curled, stretched moving from curl to stretch and vice versa, twisted, etc.

14. *Apparatus:* double bars on Nos. 4 and 14, inclined form on bottom
    bar and mat.
    Work through the sequence getting over the top bar by curling
round it, then move on to the form and balance in a held position
using the apparatus as you wish to do so, and then get off on to the
mat.

The height of the bars should be graded according to the
child's ability, *e.g.* tall and gifted performers work on bars
Nos. 4 and 16, small and gifted performers on Nos. 4 and 14,
tall and weak performers on Nos. 4 and 13, and small and
weak performers on Nos. 4 and 12.

15. *Apparatus:* double bars on Nos. 1 (turned over) and 11, inclined
    form on bar No. 1 and mat (Fig. 9).
    1. Move up the inclined form, along the bar or bars and on to the
mat.

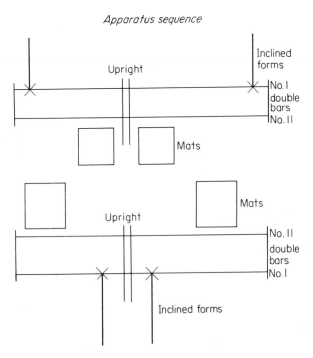

Fig. 9.

2. Move along the sequence and when dealing with the bar work use the top bar only, or the top and bottom bar, or move between the bars, staying on them whilst doing so, in order to get a variety of ways in dealing with the bar work.

3. Move the bars on to Nos. 5 and 16 and again work out a variety of ways of using them as you work through the sequence, for example, go through the bars from side to side using one or both bars and the floor to do so. As an alternative method, use the top and bottom bar alternately by using the bottom bar to help you reach the top one, and the floor to help you reach the bottom one—the form can also be used to facilitate movement.

4. When getting along the bars or working on them use different effort actions, *e.g.* pushing, pulling, swinging or a combination of these.

5. When working with the bar bring different parts of the body into contact with it, *e.g.* hands or feet moving first, or moving· with one hand on the top and one hand on the bottom bar, or moving with legs close to or away from the rest of the body.

6. When working with the bar use or make different body shapes, *e.g.* the body curled, or stretched, or moving from one shape to the other, etc.

7. Find a variety of ways of getting off the bar on to the mat, *e.g.* by using both bars or one only, with hands/feet touching the mat first, by using one or two hands on the bottom bar, or by using legs in different positions—stretching or curling them, etc.

16. *Apparatus:* saddle on bar No. 4 and mat, knotted double ropes and mat, inclined form on bar No. 4 and mat (Fig. 10).

1. Work through the sequence with hands/feet touching the mats first as you deal with both the saddle and with the inclined form.

2. Work through the sequence stretching the body as much as possible as you do so.

3. When dealing with the double ropes find different ways of getting *through* them.

4. As you deal with the saddle and inclined form, find ways of making the body go from curl to stretch shape.

5. Find ways of taking weight on hands as you go through the saddle.

6. Find different ways of balancing in a held position on the double ropes.

17. *Apparatus:* saddle on bar No. 4 and mat, form inclined on knotted double ropes and mat, double bars on Nos. 2 and 8 and mat (Fig. 11).

1. Work through the sequence with hands/feet touching the mats first when dealing with this particular piece of apparatus.

2. Include a held position of balance on the ropes and double bars in your sequence.

Apparatus sequence

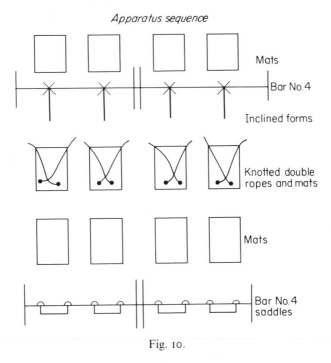

Fig. 10.

3. Work through the sequence with legs close to or away from the body all the way.

4. Work through the sequence with body stretched all the way.

18. *Apparatus:* double bars on Nos. 5 and 15 with a saddle on both bars and mat, double ropes knotted at the base and mat if required, double bars on Nos. 5 and 15 with a saddle on the bottom bar and mat (Fig. 12).

1. When working on the double bars with a saddle on both bars, find ways of taking weight on hands, *e.g.* handstand off.

2. When working on the knotted double ropes find ways of swinging in a position of held balance, then take weight on hands to get off on to mat or floor, *e.g.* swing in reverse hanging—still holding on with feet, release hands to handstand off on to mat or floor.

It is necessary here to point out to or remind the children of the impact necessary to get on to the ropes and achieve swing. This impact can be achieved by either stepping, jumping

Apparatus sequence

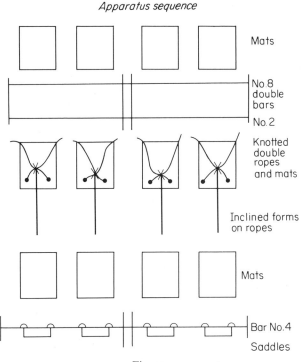

Fig. 11.

or running on to the ropes. The balance on the ropes must be in a definite held stationary position and getting off the ropes on to the floor or mat can be achieved either by complete (immediate) or by partial (delayed) transference of weight.

3. After having transferred weight from the ropes, now work out ways of transferring weight back on again. It may be necessary for another performer to catch, hold or steady the ropes to facilitate movement.

4. When working on the double bars with a saddle on the bottom bar, make use of mat to find ways of taking weight on hands and putting in a twist as well.

19. *Apparatus:* inclined form on bar No. 5, mat, a gap or space for floorwork, straight form up to box (Fig. 13).

1. Move up the inclined form keeping on it the whole time.

2. Find ways of taking weight on hands as you get off the form on to the mat.

3. "Bridge the gap" or cope with the floorwork in any way you like.
4. Move along the straight form keeping on it the whole time.
5. Get on to the box with hands first and feet following.
6. Find ways of getting off the box with a body stretch.

Apparatus sequence

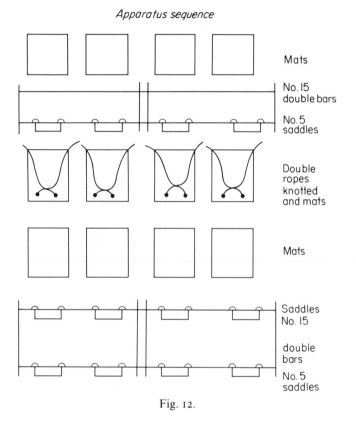

Mats

No. 15
double bars

No. 5
saddles

Double
ropes
knotted
and mats

Mats

Saddles
No. 15

double
bars

No. 5
saddles

Fig. 12.

20. *Apparatus:* inclined form on bar No. 4, mat, horse and mat or bar box and mat or box and mat or buck and mat, inclined form on bar No. 4 and mat (Fig. 14).

1. Free choice of sequence.

2. When dealing with the apparatus hands or feet to touch the mat first as you leave it.

3. Work through the whole sequence stretching legs and then stretching all the body.

4. Find ways of taking weight on hands when getting off the forms.

5. Find ways of getting on and off the apparatus, stretching the body.

Apparatus sequence

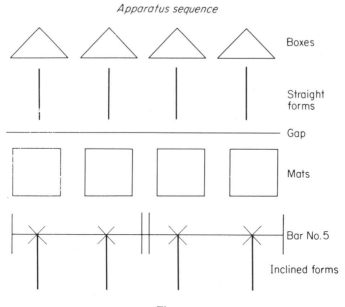

Boxes

Straight forms

Gap

Mats

Bar No. 5

Inclined forms

Fig. 13.

21. *Apparatus:* inclined form on bar No. 4, and mat, horse and mat or box and mat or inclined form on bar box and mat or buck and mat, inclined form on bar No. 4 and mat (Fig. 15).

   1. Work through the sequence with hands or feet touching the mats first.

   2. When dealing with the inclined forms find ways of using hands and feet together.

   3. Find ways of taking weight on hands when using the forms and the big apparatus, *e.g.* box, buck, etc.

   4. Work through the whole sequence with body stretching all the way.

   5. Repeat the same activity on both forms.

22. *Apparatus:* inclined form on bar No. 5, mat, gap for floorwork, and the choice of one of the following: form up to box and mat, or beating up to bar box and mat, or straight form up to horse and mat or double forms, one on top of the other, and mat (Fig. 16).

   1. Free experimental sequence down the apparatus.

   2. When dealing with the inclined form find ways of keeping on it all the time.

   3. Find ways of getting off the inclined form by taking weight on hands.

4. "Bridge the gap" or cope with the floorwork in any way you choose.

5. When moving on to the big apparatus find ways of doing so by taking weight on hands and then transferring it on to feet.

6. As you get off all apparatus find ways of stretching the body—how many shapes can you make with a stretched body?

Apparatus sequence

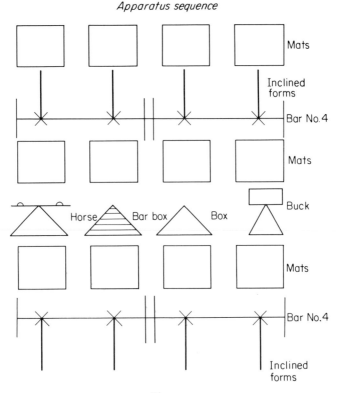

Fig. 14.

23. *Apparatus:* form up to box and mat, or beating board up to bar box and mat, or buck and double mats (two sets) for choice of apparatus (Fig. 17).

1. Free experimental choice when working on apparatus.

2. When getting over apparatus find ways of doing so with hands or feet touching the mat first.

3. Find ways of getting over the apparatus stretching legs and/or body.

4. Get on the apparatus and then off again, taking weight on to hands and then feet to get on, and finding a variety of ways to get off.

Apparatus sequence

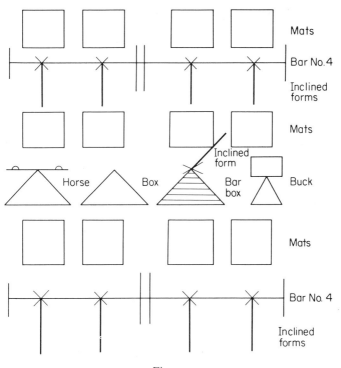

Fig. 15.

Apparatus tasks

The class mainly work in groups performing a sequence of movement on one, two or three pieces of apparatus—different pieces of apparatus being used by different groups (unlike apparatus sequences, where all the class use the same apparatus), and these pieces being placed in different positions in the gymnasium.

TASK ONE

1. The class work on mats. Get over the mat in as many different ways as you can, *e.g.* roll, jump, cartwheel, etc.

2. Now think about the different directions you can use as well as developing a variety of ideas.

3. In a space, on the floor, find different ways of curling and stretching the body.

4. Go back to working on the mat using different ways of transferring weight in different directions, on different levels making different body shapes.

5. Select one way and practise it—practise the body shape on the floor whilst awaiting a turn on the mat.

Apparatus sequence

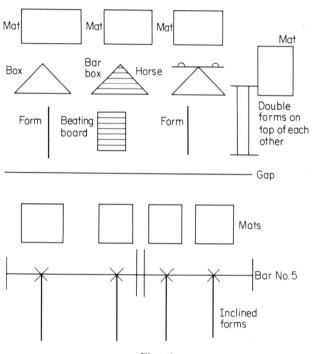

Fig. 16.

TASK TWO

1. On mats as before, get up to, over and away from the mat using the same idea or transference of weight as you do all this. Find a variety of sequences.

2. Select three ways to do this and practise them.

3. Practise the body shapes of the three selected ways or sequences on the floor whilst waiting for a turn on the mat.

Apparatus sequence

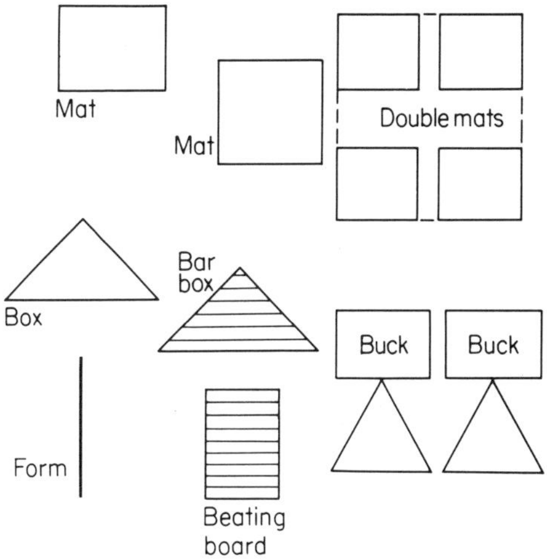

Fig. 17.

TASK THREE

1. On mats as before, get up to, over, and away from the mat using the same idea or transference of weight to get up to and away from the mat, and a different idea or transference of weight to get over it. Then select three sequences doing this and practise them.

2. Get up to, over, and away from the mat using a different idea or transference of weight to do all three actions. Select three sequences as before and practise them.

TASK FOUR

Using different pieces of apparatus combined together, the task is continuous movement down the line of apparatus. The following are examples of sequences:

1. Inclined form on bar No. 7, mat, horse, mat, inclined form on another piece of apparatus of choice (Fig. 18a).

2. Flat form up to bar, mat, box either way and mat (Fig. 18b).

3. Flat form up to box with ropes mid-way along box to lie each side of it and mat (Fig. 18c).

Here a specific task is introduced when dealing with the box, i.e. to get on to it and to balance on the ropes in a held position before continuing off.

4. Incline a form any height on the ribstalls and fix the other end on to some piece of big apparatus. Here it is necessary to make sure that the flat end of the form is resting on the big apparatus (Fig. 19).

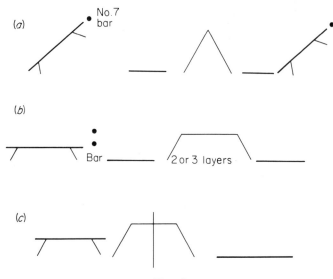

Fig. 18.

Do not rest the form on its end support but let that push into the side of the big apparatus. Some very creative ways of getting off the big apparatus can be found, especially when the horse is used.

    5. Inclined forms on rope ladders or on knotted ropes.

    6. Inclined forms on window ladder, bars (high and low), horse and wall bar or buck and wall bar or box and wall bar (Fig. 19). Here the specific task of finding various different ways of getting up the form, *e.g.* pulling, rolling, etc., is introduced. This leads to finding ways of continuing to climb and descend via the form, or to ways of balancing in a held position on the apparatus with the body completely without contact with the form.

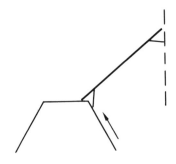

Fig. 19.

7. Any two pieces of apparatus placed reasonably near each other, *e.g.* horse and ribstall (Fig. 20), or bar on No. 12 with two or three sections of the box, or form with buck, etc. Here the specific task is to get the *whole* body from being completely on the first piece of apparatus to being completely on the second piece of apparatus without touching the floor, for example:

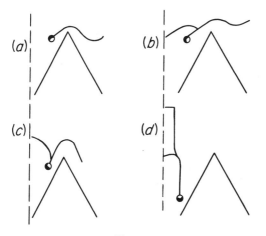

Fig. 20.

(*a*) on arriving backwards on the horse, balance there in a held position;
(*b*) lean over into overgrasp position;
(*c*) get close in——head down facing the ribstall;
(*d*) a violent kick lifts to reverse hanging on ribstall *facing* the ribstall.

One can then progress to different methods of getting on and off as well as developing the transition method of getting from one piece of apparatus to the other, for example, in the method illustrated above, in order to get off the ribstall one can hook one's toes into it to take one's weight, then put hands on the floor and descend in a transference of weight.

8. Here again the specific task is the same as in (7) but the apparatus is the bar combined with the box (Fig. 21), for example:

(*a*) run to spring on bar and balance there;
(*b*) lean forward and down to reach the box;
(*c*) walk hands along;
(*d*) walk feet on to the box——hold with seat high in the air;
(*e*) continue off the box on to the floor.

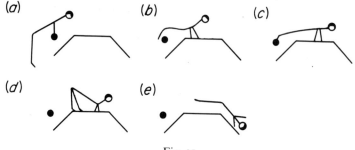

Fig. 21.

9. Here again the specific task is the same as in (7) and (8) but the apparatus is two forms combined with the buck (Fig. 22). For example:

(a) crawl along with feet on one form and hands on the other; pause half-way along for a held balance position and then continue as before;

(b) on reaching the buck, transfer weight on to it by turning and getting on with feet going first;

(c) when body weight has been completely transferred on to the buck, arch body in a balance position and then continue off on to the floor.

In apparatus tasks (7)–(9) transition movements are necessary in order to get into positions or balances required. These should be allowed provided that they *are* necessary and are

(a)

(b)

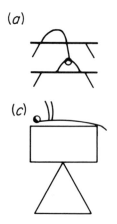

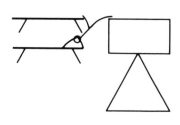

Fig. 22.

smooth and in keeping with the held position of balance. Provided that the children answer the question, movement task or problem set and work to their capability and fullest capacity, a considerable leeway should be allowed and plenty of room for experiment. Give them a broad directive if a task is to be set, or give them free experimentation with the apparatus itself providing sufficient task, and then coach the children in individual performance or specific points relating to the work of the whole class. If, as the teacher, you find a good idea or apparatus arrangement, or if a child in one particular class finds one, it is often a good plan to work it through the school regardless of age of the children. The modern method lends itself to this and obviously the older and more skilful children get a different result from the younger or less able. It is amazing how differently classes interpret the same apparatus, and often from this the teacher is more able to assess individual needs.

TASK FIVE

Here the apparatus consists of double bars, with low box, horse and mats if necessary. A different or identical task is set for each different piece of large apparatus, for example, when dealing with the bars find ways of approaching them with a run in order to get up and over them—gate vault, etc. Before leaving the bars, balance there with legs in various positions, leave by swinging legs into space in various ways in order to so leave. When dealing with the box, find ways of running up to and over it, for example, run into a sideways body position on the box with one hand holding the box propping weight on shoulder, and the other hand either on the floor, or against the box or holding the other side of box for support, keeping the head well to one side. Balance there with legs in various positions and continue off on to the floor with legs reaching into space in different ways.

TASK SIX

Using the box longways find different ways of running up and over as before. This can be done either as a continuous vault getting straight into position and off, or by getting on, then into position and off, or with a held balance in between by getting straight into position of balance—holding it there and then off, or by getting on, then into position of balance—holding it there and then off. An example of this is the method of approach and body position as described in Task Five, or running into an elbow stand or hand or headstand on the box, or by getting on to the box first and then into these various positions. One can then continue off with the backwards or forwards splits of legs, or by balancing in a head, hand, or elbow stand with feet close to head in a held position and then continue over and off the other end of the box.

TASK SEVEN

Using the horse with pommels, the box and the buck longways, find different ways of getting on (from a run or a standstill) and then get off again the same way that you got on. For example, from a run or standstill, head, hand or elbowstand against the apparatus, into a knee grip with leg parting to get on, arching the back and pulling at the same time, then go back in reverse to get off. A held position of balance can be included in between getting on and off.

TASK EIGHT

Free movement sequence on the apparatus sequence (Fig. 23)—one can start and finish at either end.

TASK NINE

Find ways of hanging in various positions with weight taken on different parts of the body with different body parts holding on to the ropes, *e.g.* hanging upside down—hold with feet and neck (against knot)—arms stretched out (Fig. 24).

TASK TEN

Free movement sequence on combined apparatus (Fig. 25).

TASK ELEVEN

Free movement sequence on combined apparatus (Fig. 26).

TASK TWELVE

Figure 27 shows simple apparatus combinations with or without spaces between apparatus. Free experiment on these combinations.

TASK THIRTEEN

Figure 28 shows compound apparatus combinations. Free experiment on these combinations.

Figure 28c can be varied by:

1. a gap between the box and the bar or
2. a saddle on X or
3. use of the top bar also or
4. the bottom bar low or high.

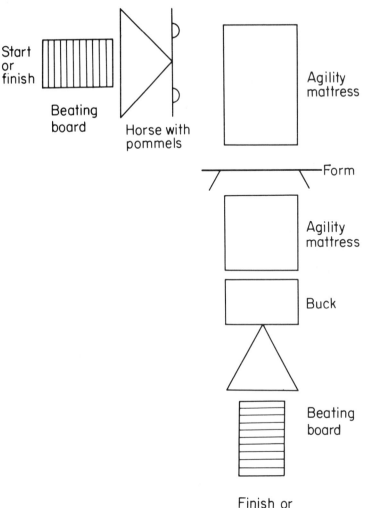

Start or finish

Beating board

Horse with pommels

Agility mattress

Form

Agility mattress

Buck

Beating board

Finish or start

Fig. 23.

On apparatus work the *floor* is also important. We must get (start) from the floor on to the apparatus and end on the floor. Children should not be allowed to ignore this factor. Leaving gaps between pieces of apparatus can lead to link up of the floorwork with the apparatus work.

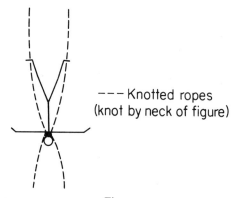

--- Knotted ropes
(knot by neck of figure)

Fig. 24.

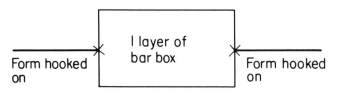

Fig. 25.

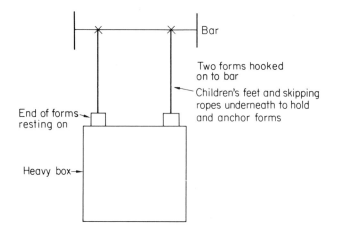

Fig. 26.

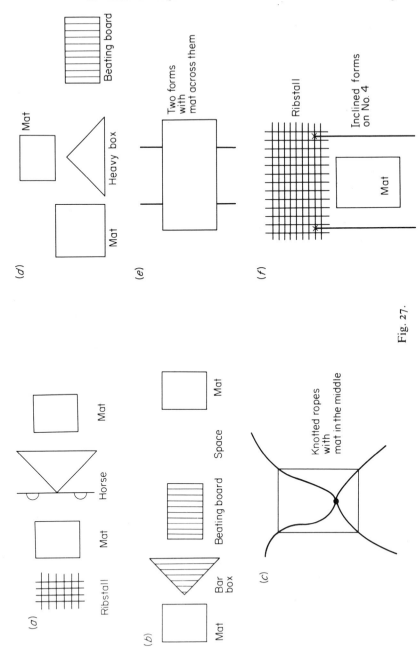

Fig. 27.

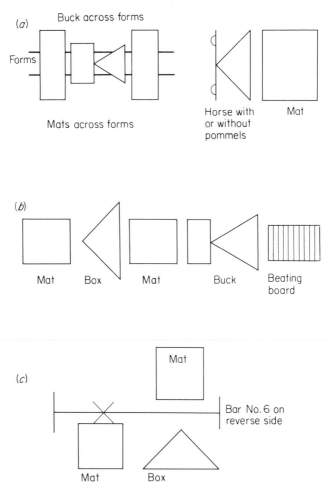

Fig. 28.

Chapter Seven

EDUCATIONAL GYMNASTICS: III

WORKING ON APPARATUS

Activities on apparatus are concerned with weight control. They can involve continuous transference of weight or can be interrupted for purposes of held balance in a position. There is an approach to the apparatus, the actual activity, and a finish to the work. The approach is concerned with moving along or from the floor to the apparatus or up to it, the activity is the way of dealing with the apparatus, which in turn leads one from the apparatus to the floor again, with a subsequent transference of weight along the floor or mat in order to achieve a finish to the work.

When working on apparatus a variety of actions should be used. The following are examples of these actions:

1. On and off.
2. On and along to off.
3. Up to balance and off.
4. On, up to balance and off.
5. On and along and off.
6. Along.
7. Over.
8. Through and over.
9. Over and through.
10. On, through and off.
11. Over and through and off.

These actions can be performed using a change of direction, for example, get on forwards and off backwards; a change of approach to the apparatus, for example, use the box longways or widthways; and a change of bodyshape, for example, a twist on the apparatus. A variety of body parts should be used to take and transfer weight when dealing with the apparatus, and different levels in space should also be used, for example, body close to or away from the apparatus. Different preparations can be used for flight purposes, for example, a running, stepping or jumping take-off, depending upon the time element involved. A change of speed should be evident, but this again depends upon whether the child wishes to move in a quick or sustained manner, and upon which time element can best be used to facilitate the actual performing of the activity. Some children can best perform by employing a fast speed, whilst others with great control of body weight can perform difficult movements in a very sustained manner. The ideal, of course, is to have mastery of both. Also evident should be a change in the actual usage of the apparatus, for example, the single use of a particular piece or the repeated use of same either with or without severing the contact of body with apparatus.

The following are ideas produced by children on various pieces of apparatus. For the benefit of readers of varied training and experience they have been described using the language for formal vaults and have also been described by the transference of weight used. Children usually describe their work by transference of weight purposes or invent their own names, for example, shouldersault. They tend to refer to activities which require a running preparation as "springs," and to those which require an on the spot preparation as "stands." A description of shape has been given broadly in terms of stretch or curl or a combination of both, but it must be noted that legs may be in various positions with regard to near to and far away from one another and to the rest of the body.

It may be rare, but it is possible for children to perform twisted movements in a stretched as well as a curled position. A movement is deemed to be a curl when the appendages, or arms and legs, are close to the rest of the body; and a stretch when they are far away from it, but it is also possible to stretch with arms and legs close to the rest of the body.

ACTIVITIES ON APPARATUS

Activities on the box

Here a variety of number of layers can be used and the box can be in a longways or widthways position.

1. Crouch jump on to the box and either an extension jump or a forward roll off. Here the transference of weight is from hands to feet to get on, and from feet to feet to get off, or from hands to shoulders to back to seat to feet. The body shape moves from curl to stretch, or from curl to curl (Plate 8).

Plate 8

2. Jump on and jump off with either a tuck or extension jump. Here the transference of weight is from feet to feet with the body shape moving from curl to curl or curl to stretch, etc.

3. Handstand or headstand on with leg parting to grip the sides of the box (Plates 9 and 10), and either handstand or headstand off (Plates 11 and 12). Here the transference of weight is from either hands, or head and hands, to legs astride to get on, and from hands, or head and hands, to feet to get off. The body shape moves from stretch through curl to stretch again.

4. Crouch jump on and cartwheel off (Plate 13). Here the transference of weight is from hands to feet to get on, and from hands to feet to get off. The body shape moves from curl to stretch.

Plate 9   Plate 10

Plate 11   Plate 12

Plate 13

Plate 14

Plate 15   Plate 16

5. Jump into prone lying on front of body on the box (Plate 14) and continue off by a handstand or headstand (Plates 15 and 16). Here the transference of weight is from hands to the front of the body to get on, and continues from hands, or hands and head, to feet to get off. The body shape moves from stretch to stretch. The box is used longways.

6. Again using the box longways, jump on with a backward roll to get straight off (Plate 17). Here the transference of weight is from feet to seat to back to shoulders to hands to feet to get on and straight off. The body shape moves from curl to curl with leg stretching to get off if required.

7. Using the box longways crouch jump on, leading into a forward rocking movement on the front of the body (Plate 18), continuing off forward with the body in a position of curl with the feet touching the head, and with a subsequent landing on feet. Here the transference of weight is from hands to feet to get on, and from hands to shoulders to tummy to thighs for the rocking movement, leading to tummy to shoulders and hands to feet to continue off. The body shape moves from curl to curl. As an alternative a leg stretch can be used when continuing off the box (Plate 19).

Plate 17

Plate 18

Plate 19

8. Crouch jump on (forwards) and crouch jump off (backwards or sideways) with legs curled or stretched. Here the transference of weight is from hands to feet in getting on and off, with the body shape moving from curl to curl (with legs stretched if required).

9. Jump into prone lying sideways to get on, and cartwheel off. Here the transference of weight is from hands to the side of the body to get on, and from hands to feet to get off. The body shape moves from stretch to stretch.

10. Using the box widthways, jump into prone lying on the front of the body to get on, leading into a forward rocking on the front of the body and continue off (Plate 20). Here the

Plate 20

transference of weight is from hands to the front of the body to get on, leading into transference of weight from hands to shoulders to tummy to thighs back to tummy to shoulders to hands to feet to continue off. The body can move through a variety of curl and stretch shapes as desired.

11. Again using the box widthways, jump into prone lying on the front of the body, with one hand on the box and one hand on the floor, and continue off with either a cartwheel or a handstand (Plates 21 and 22). The transference of weight is from hands to the front of the body to get on, and continues from either the side of the body to hands to feet in a cartwheel, or from hands to feet in a handstand, to get off. The body shape moves from stretch to stretch.

Plate 21

Plate 22

12. Using the box longways, crouch jump on with an elbow stand off (Plate 23). Here the transference of weight is from hands to feet to get on, and from elbows and forearms to feet to get off. The body shape moves from curl to stretch.

13. Using the box longways, backward squat on leading into headstand backwards to get off (Plate 24). Here the transference of weight is from hands to seat to get on, and from hands and head to feet to get off. The body shape moves from curl to stretch.

Plate 23

Plate 24

Plate 25

Plate 26

14. Crouch jump on and handstand with sideways screw off—note the transference of weight here from two hands to one (Plates 25 and 26). The transference of weight is from hands to feet to get on, and from two hands to one hand, to feet to get off. The body shape moves from curl to stretch.

15. Using the box longways, crouch jump on with a forward roll along and off. The transference of weight is from hands to feet to get on, and from hands to shoulders to back to seat to feet to continue along and off. The body shape moves from curl to curl with legs stretched if desired to get off.

16. Using the box longways, up to balance position to get on. Balance on hands and shoulder girdle (sideways position to the box) with one hand on the floor (Plate 27). To get off

Plate 27

continue with either a forward roll or a handstand off the side of the box. The transference of weight is from hands and shoulder girdle in position of balance, to either shoulder to

back to seat to feet in a somersault off, or to feet if a handstand off is used. The body shape moves from stretch to curl
or stretch to stretch.

17. Using the box longways, up to balance position to get
on. Balance on hands and shoulder girdle (sideways position
to the box) with knee prop. The whole body is therefore on the
box (Plate 28). Continue in a forward roll off. The transference of weight is hands and shoulder girdle and knee in

Plate 28

position of balance, to shoulders to back to seat to feet to
get off. The body shape moves from stretch to curl with leg
stretching to off if desired.

18. Using the box longways, crouch jump on, then up to
balance position on hands and shoulder girdle (for a prop)
(Plate 29), and either handstand or forward roll off. The
transference of weight is from hands to feet to get on, then
to hands and shoulder girdle for position of balance, to
either feet, or shoulders to back to seat to get off. The body
shape moves from curl to stretch to either stretch or curl.

19. Using the box longways, crouch jump on, into forward
somersault along, into extension jump off. The transference
of weight is from hands to feet to get on, to hands to shoulders

Plate 29

to back to seat to feet to continue along, and from feet to feet to get off. The body shape moves from curl to curl to stretch.

20. Using the box longways, backward squat on, leading to backward somersault into leg parting and astride grip along the box, into handstand off. The transference of weight is from hands to seat to get on, to seat to back to shoulders to hands to legs astride along the box, to hands to feet to get off. The body shape moves from curl, to curl into stretch, to stretch.

21. Using the box longways, crouch jump on, into headstand (with legs in various positions) along the box, into roll off. Here the transference of weight is from hands to feet to get on, on to hands and head to move along, and on to shoulders to back to seat to legs to feet to get off (Plates 30, 31 and 32). The body shape moves from curl, into stretch, into curl with leg stretching if desired.

22. Backward roll along the box where the transference of weight is from hands to seat to back to shoulders to hands to feet. The body shape is curl with leg stretching if desired.

23. Forward roll along the box (Plate 33), where the transference of weight is from hands to shoulders to back

Plate 32

Plate 31

Plate 30

Plate 33

to seat to feet. Here again the body shape is curl with leg stretching if desired.

24. Using the box longways, longfly over (Plate 34), with the transference of weight from hands to feet and the body in a stretch shape.

25. Using the box longways, longfly into handspring over with the transference of weight from hands to feet and the body shape moving from one position of stretch to another.

26. Using the box longways with a beating board on top of it, either a forward somersault or extension jump off the

Plate 34

beating board into the air with subsequent landing on the floor. Here the transference of weight is from feet to feet with the body in a curl or stretch shape.

27. Using the box either longways or widthways, fence vault over (sideways). The transference of weight is from hands to feet with a leg stretching body shape.

28. Using the box widthways, backward or forward roll over. Here the transference of weight is either from hands to seat to back to shoulders to hands to feet, or from hands to shoulders to back to seat to feet. The body shape is curl with leg stretching if desired.

29. Front vault over the box (sideways) with the box longways or widthways. The transference of weight is from hands to feet with a leg stretching body shape.

30. Using the box widthways:

    (*a*) crouch jump,
    (*b*) cartwheel (Plate 35),
    (*c*) handspring (Plates 36 and 37) (with leg parting),
    (*d*) headspring (Plate 38),
    (*e*) somersault vault,
    (*f*) screw vault,
    (*g*) thief vault,
    (*h*) quick or slow squat,
    (*i*) shouldersault

over. The transference of weight in methods (*a*), (*b*), (*c*), (*e*), (*f*), (*g*), and (*h*) is from hands to feet, in (*d*) from hands and head to feet, and in (*i*) from hands and back of neck and shoulders to feet. The appropriate body shape is either curl or stretch or part curl and part stretch.

31. Using the box widthways, dive-handstand straight over, with hands reaching for the floor on the far side of the box, with or without the body touching the box. The transference of weight is from feet to hands to feet if the body does not touch the box, and from feet to tummy to hands to feet if it does. The body shape is stretch.

32. Using the box widthways, dive-cartwheel straight over, with hands reaching for the floor on the far side of the box, with or without the body touching it. The transference of

Plate 35

Plate 36

Plate 37

Plate 38

weight is from feet to hand to hand to foot to foot without the body touching the box, and from feet to side of body to hand to hand to foot to foot if it does. The body shape is stretch.

33. Headstand or handstand over using the box widthways. The head and hands, or hands, can be on the far side of the box on the floor or on the near side of the box on the floor (Plates 39, 40, and 41), or on the box itself (Plate 42). The transference of weight is either from head and hands to feet, or from hands to feet; or from head and hands to back to seat to feet, or from hands to back to seat to feet according to where the hands or head and hands are placed in relationship to the box. The body shape is stretch or moves from stretch into curl into stretch accordingly.

34. Using the box widthways, handstand over, with one hand on the box, and one hand on the floor on the far side of the box (Plate 43). The transference of weight is from hands and the front of the body on to feet with legs bent and with the body in a stretch shape.

Plate 39   Plate 40

Plate 41   Plate 42

Plate 43

Activities on the buck

These can be done with the buck widthways or longways and at variable heights.

1. Crouch jump on and extension jump off. The transference of weight is from hands to feet to get on, and from feet to feet to get off, with the body moving from curl to stretch shape.

2. Using the box longways, handstand with leg parting to grip the buck, get on arching the back to pull up to a sitting position which leads to handstand off forwards. The transference of weight is from hands to legs astride to get on, and from hands to feet to get off. The body shape moves from stretch to part curl part stretch into stretch again.

3. Jump into prone, lying on the front of the body to get on, and continue in either handstand, or headstand to get off. The transference of weight is from hands to the front of the body to get on, and from hands, or head and hands to feet, to get off. The body shape moves from one stretch position to another.

4. Jump into prone, lying on front or back of body to get on, and continue off in either a forward or backward roll. This is done using the buck widthways and necessitates holding on to the legs of the buck with the feet, or the sides of the buck with hands, to facilitate movement. The transference of weight is from hands and the front, or back, of body to feet. The body shape moves from stretch into curl with leg stretching if desired.

5. Jump into prone, lying on the front or back of the body, and continue off into handstand, into forward roll, or handstand, into backward roll to get off. The transference of weight is from hands and the front or back of body, to either hands to shoulders to back to seat to feet, or hands to shoulders and back to hands to feet. The body shape is from stretch to stretch to curl with leg stretching if desired.

6. Using the buck widthways, jump into prone lying on back of body, and continue off in handstand, or headstand backwards. The transference of weight is from hands to the back of body to get on, and from either hands, or head and

hands, to feet to get off. The body shape moves from stretch to stretch.

7. Using the buck widthways, jump into prone lying on side of body to get on, and continue off in a cartwheel. The transference of weight is from hands to the side of the body to get on, and from hand to hand to foot to foot to get off. The body shape moves from stretch to stretch.

8. Using the buck widthways, jump into prone lying on the front of the body, with one hand holding on to the buck, and the other one on the floor. This leads into a body twist and cartwheel off. The transference of weight is from hands to the front of the body and hands to get on, to hand to foot to foot to get off. The body shape moves from stretch to stretch.

9. Using the buck widthways, jump into astride sitting to get on, leading into flight off, with forward stretching of legs and a good push from hands to assist flight. The transference weight is from hands to legs astride and seat to get on, and from hands to feet to get off. The body shape moves from stretch to stretch.

10. Using the buck widthways, backward squat to get on, with a swizzle round leading into flight off, with legs stretching forward and a good push from hands to assist flight. The transference of weight is from hands to seat to get on, and from seat to hands to feet to get off. The body shape moves from stretch to stretch.

11. Using the buck widthways, jump into prone lying forwards, leading into a swizzle round on front of body, leading into flight off, with legs stretching backwards and a strong push from hands to assist flight. The transference of weight is from hands to the front of the body to get on, and from there on to feet to get off. The body shape moves from stretch to stretch.

12. Crouch jump on and crouch jump off with legs in various positions. The transference of weight is from hands to feet to get on and off and the body shape is curled with legs making various shapes (stretched or curled) as desired.

13. Jump on and off. The transference of weight is from feet to feet and the body shape can be various as desired.

14. Using the buck longways, crouch jump on and cartwheel off. The transference of weight is from hands to feet to get on, and hand to hand to foot to foot to get off. The body shape moves from curl to stretch.

15. Using the buck longways, jump into backward squat on, and continue in a backward roll off. The transference of weight is from hands to seat to get on, and from hands to shoulders to feet to get off. The body shape moves from stretch into curl with leg stretching.

16. Using the buck longways, forward roll along. The transference of weight is from hands to shoulders to back to seat to feet with the body shape moving from curl into leg stretching.

17. Leapfrog over (Plate 44). The transference of weight is from hands to feet with the body in a stretch shape.

Plate 44

18. Using the buck widthways, somersault vault over. The transference of weight is from hands to feet, with the body in a curl shape. Leg stretching during flight before landing can be added if desired.

19. Using the buck widthways, handspring or head-spring (Plate 45) over. The transference of weight is from hands, or hands and head, to feet with the body in a stretch shape.

20. Crouch jump over with transference of weight from hands to feet and body in a curl shape.

21. Using the buck longways, longfly, or longfly into hand-spring, over. The transference of weight is from hands to feet with the body in a stretch shape.

22. Using the buck widthways, shouldersault over (Plate 46). The transference of weight is from hands and shoulders and back of neck to feet. The body shape is partly curled with legs stretching.

23. Fence vault over with a sideways approach. The transference of weight is from hands to feet with the body in a stretch shape.

24. Front vault over with a sideways approach. The transference of weight is from hands to feet with the body in a stretch shape.

Plate 45

Plate 46

Plate 47   Plate 48

25. Using the buck widthways, handstand over, with hands holding the sides of the buck (Plate 47). The transference of weight is from hands and shoulder girdle to feet with the body in a stretch shape.

26. Using the buck widthways, quick squat over with transference of weight from hands to feet and the body in a leg curl to stretch shape.

27. Dive handstand forwards over the buck, using it widthways, with hands reaching for the floor on the far side of it (Plate 48). The transference of weight is from feet to tummy to hands to feet with the body in a stretch shape.

28. Using the buck widthways, dive cartwheel over, with hands reaching for the floor on the far side of the buck. The transference of weight is from feet to the side of the body, to hand to hand to foot to foot with the body in a stretch shape.

29. Using the buck widthways, handstand over, with one hand on the buck, and one hand on the floor on the far side of it. The transference of weight is from hands and the front of body, to feet with the body in a stretch shape.

Activities on the horse

These can be performed with the horse widthways or longways at variable heights and with or without the pommels.

1. (*a*) Crouch jump forwards on to the end of the horse, leading into handstand off backwards, off the other end with hands on the pommels, and a good leg lift to assist flight. Here we have a change of direction. The transference of weight is from hands to feet to get on and off with the body moving from curl to stretch shape.

(*b*) Crouch jump forwards on to the middle of the horse, leading into handstand off forwards, with hands on the pommels of the horse. Here we have no change of direction. The transference of weight is from hands to feet to get on and off with the body moving from curl to stretch shape.

2. Crouch jump on to the end of the horse, and handstand off sideways (Plate 49). The horse is used without the pommels and the transference of weight is from hands to feet to get on and off with the body moving from curl to stretch shape.

Plate 49

3. Crouch jump on and extension jump off. The transference of weight is from hands to feet to get on, and from feet to feet to get off. The body shape moves from curl to stretch.

4. (a) Jump into prone lying on the front of the body to get on, leading into handstand or headstand off forwards with the body passing through the pommels. The transference of weight is from hands to the front of the body to get on, and from hands, or hands and head, to feet to get off. The body moves from one stretched shape to another.

(b) Backward squat to get on, leading into handstand or headstand off backwards with the body passing through the pommels. The transference of weight is from hands to seat to get on, and from hands, or hands and head, to feet to get off. The body shape moves from curl into stretch.

5. Crouch jump forwards on to the horse, and by a turn swizzle round, leading into jump off backwards, with leg lift and stretch to assist flight, with the body passing through and with the hands holding on to the pommels. Here there is a change of direction. The transference of weight is from hands to feet to get on and off with the body moving from curl to stretch shape.

6. Jump on and off going through the pommels. The transference of weight is from feet to feet to get on and off with the body in various shapes.

7. Flight on to horse, with hands on the pommels, and one knee on the horse, with the other leg stretching backwards to get on, leading into handstand over, with a good push from hands and knee, and a kick from backward stretched leg to assist flight. The transference of weight is from hands and one knee, to hands and feet with the body shape moving from stretch to stretch.

8. Moving through and over the horse:

(a) somersault,
(b) quick squat,
(c) slow squat (Plate 50),
(d) thief,
(e) wolf.

Plate 50

Here the transference of weight is from hands to feet with the body in various shapes of curl or stretch or part curl part stretch.

9. With or without the pommels, handspring or headspring through and over, in a forwards or sideways direction (Plates 51, 52 and 53). The transference of weight is from hands, or hands and head, to feet with the body in a stretch shape.

10. Shouldersault through and over, leading into flip-flap off (back arched, legs stretching to reach up and out and down). This can be held as a balance before flight off (Plate 54). The transference of weight is from hands and shoulders and back of neck, to feet with the body moving from curl to stretch shape.

11. Handstand through and over. This can be done with hands holding underneath the body of the horse (Plate 55) or with one hand under the horse and the other reaching over the horse finishing with the reaching hand on the mat and the other hand sliding over the top of the horse (Plate 56). The transference of weight is from hands to front of body to

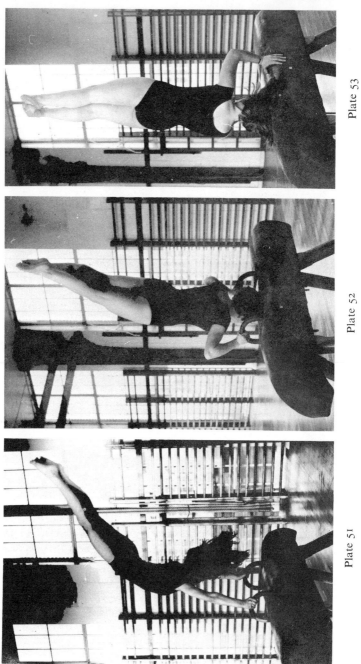

Plate 51

Plate 52

Plate 53

Plate 54

Plate 55

Plate 56

feet, or from one hand to front of body to the other hand to feet. The body shape is stretched.

12. Dive handstand forwards, going over and through, with hands reaching for the floor on the far side of the horse (Plate 57). The transference of weight is from feet to tummy to hands to feet with the body in a stretch shape.

Plate 57   Plate 58

13. Dive cartwheel sideways, going over and through, with hands reaching for the floor on the far side of the horse (Plate 58). The transference of weight is from feet to side of body to hand to hand to foot to foot with the body in a stretch shape.

14. (a) Reverse hanging on the near side of the horse, going over and through and off (Plate 59). The transference of weight is from hands to back to seat to feet with the body in a stretch shape.

(b) Jump into prone lying on tummy, leading into reverse hanging on the far side of the horse, going through,

Plate 59   Plate 60

over and off (Plate 60). The transference of weight is from hands to tummy to front of body to feet with the body in a stretch shape.

15. Prone lying forwards or backwards, to forward or backward somersault to go over, through and off. The transference of weight is from hands to tummy to feet, or from hands to back of body to feet with the body shape moving from stretch to curl with leg stretching if desired.

16. Flight into forward sitting, leading into flight off, with legs stretching forward, and a strong push from hands and seat to facilitate this, in order to get on, through and off the horse. The transference of weight is from hands to seat to get on, and from hands to feet to get through and off. The body shape can be performed with various leg stretches.

17. Prone lying on the front of the body (Plate 61). This leads into a forward rocking movement, with feet close to head position, which in turn leads to a handstand, going through and off the horse. The transference of weight is

from hands to the front of the body to get on, and from hands
and the front of the body to feet to get through and off. The
body shapes passes from stretch to curl to stretch.

Plate 61

18. Crouch jump to get on to the end of the horse, which
leads into a forward shouldersault, to get through the pommels
and off. Here there is a change of direction. The transference
of weight is from hands to feet to get on, and from hands and
shoulders to feet to get through and off. The body shape
moves from curl to curl with leg stretching.

19. Crouch jump to get on to the end of the horse, leading
into a forward somersault, to get through the pommels and
off. Here there is a change of direction (Plates 62 and 63).
The transference of weight is from hands to feet to get on,
and from hands to shoulders to back to feet to get through
and off. The body shape moves from curl to curl with leg
stretching if desired.

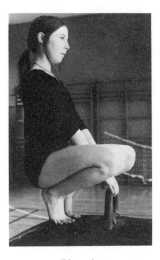

Plate 62

Plate 63

20. Prone lying on side of body to get on to the horse, leading into cartwheel, with hands reaching for the floor on the far side of the horse, to get through and off. The transference of weight is from hands to the side of the body to get on, and from hand to hand to foot to foot to get through and off, with the body in a stretch shape.

21. Prone lying on the front of the body to get on, leading into a cartwheel, either with hands on the floor on the far side of the horse, or with one hand on the floor and the other hand on the pommel of the horse. The transference of weight is from hands to the front of the body to get on, and from hand to hand to foot to foot to get through and over, or from one hand to foot to foot. The body shape moves from stretch to stretch.

22. Handstand or headstand, into legs astride grip on to one end of the horse, arching the back to pull up to sitting position with hands on the pommels. Handstand or headstand off the neck end of the horse (Plates 64 and 65). The transference of weight is from hands, or hands and head, to seat and legs astride and hands to get on, and from seat and legs astride to hands, or hands and head, to feet to get off. The body shape is stretch to stretch position.

Plate 64   Plate 65

23. Crouch jump forward on to horse, to land in the middle of the pommels, leading into forward somersault off one end (Plates 66, 67 and 68). Here there is a change of direction in the use of the horse. The transference of weight is from hands to feet to hands to shoulders to back to seat to feet and the body shape moves from curl to curl with leg stretching.

24. Crouch jump forward on to horse to land in the middle of the pommels as before (one pommel having been removed). This leads into headstand, into forward roll off one end (Plate 69). Here there is a change of direction again in the use of the horse which can be with or without pommels. The transference of weight is from hands to feet to hands and head to shoulders to back to seat to feet. The body shape moves from curl to stretch to curl with leg stretching.

25. Backward squat on to one end of the horse, which leads into a backward somersault, with leg lift (Plate 70) in order to arrive in backward astride sitting, in the middle of the horse. The transference of weight is from hands to seat to hands and shoulders to hands and seat and legs astride. The body moves from curl to curl with leg stretching to curling.

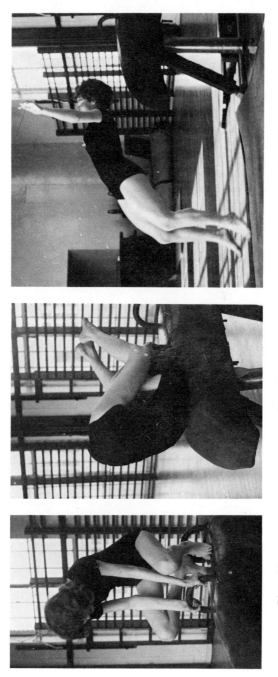

Plate 68

Plate 67

Plate 66

Plate 69

Plate 70

26. (*a*) Crouch jump,
    (*b*) screw vault
sideways over the horse. The transference of weight is from hands to feet with the body in a curl shape.

27. Leapfrog over the horse with legs astride the pommels or with both legs to one side. The transference of weight is from hands to feet with the body in a stretch shape.

PORTABLE APPARATUS AND APPARATUS IMPROVEMENTS OR ADDITIONS

Portable apparatus in a gymnasium should include eight saddles, at least twenty-four forms of various widths, an equal number of mats of various sizes, six boxes, four bucks, six horses with an equal number of beating or spring-boards, eight "tiger" stools and four catching or safety nets. Apparatus improvements could be made by the adoption of much wider forms with padded surfaces, and with three bars or beams instead of the usual two with fixed and travelling uprights. Here again the width of the bars or beams could be varied.

The introduction of "body-bouncers" (the author's design: a harness or belt with elasticated ropes attached at either side coupling the child to an overhead support which may be fixed or movable; this would counteract gravity, allowing the child to perform agility movements in the air) would greatly assist flight and weight control, as would attachments to hook on to ropes into which body parts could fit, for example, loops for neck, wrists and feet. Hooks which would anchor ropes to the floor would also be an additional advantage. The inclusion of catching or landing nets such as trapeze and high wire artistes use would assist the growth of confidence and prevent serious accidents and in addition promote flight movements such as somersaults and flip-flaps in the air.

"Tiger" stools (the author's design: a form of padded stool similar to those used in a circus by performing tigers or commonly employed as bar stools, of adjustable height and varying shape, some having adjustable surfaces like the loose-leaf dining-room table) would assist in providing a different challenge and enlarge movement and apparatus vocabulary.

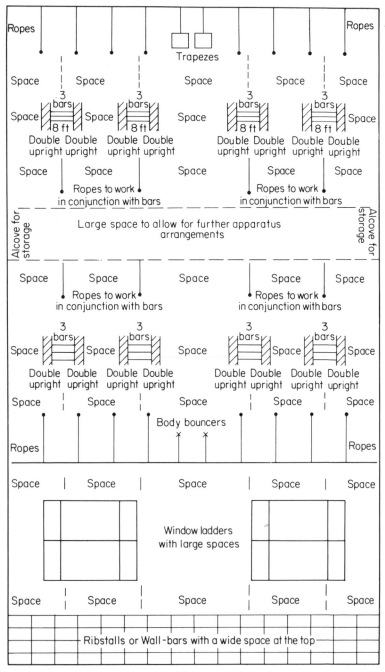

Fig. 29.

The above portable apparatus and additions and improvements to same are incorporated in a gymnasium specially designed for movement purposes. A plan of this is shown in Fig. 29.

Chapter Eight

EDUCATIONAL DANCE

INTRODUCTION

Educational dance should be creative and expressive. It is concerned with the mastery of movement and the development of the child's personality, acting as a vehicle for it. Ideas, expression (of face and body), appreciation of rhythm and standards of performance are important in this work, which should also provide opportunity for individual partner and group work or participation. There are two factors of supreme importance in educational dance: that the work is expressed in the *face* as well as in the body, and that it is concerned with an inner attitude and an inner concentration as well as an outward physical expression—an outward, visible sign of an inward feeling and thought. In dance we have to look, think, listen, move and feel. These are the necessary elements of a successful lesson without which there cannot be the utmost involvement and participation. Dance requires the participation and involvement in close harmony of almost all the child's senses.

The task of writing about dance is a difficult one—only guiding principles can be given as dance is concerned with personal attributes and sensitivity. One cannot say with conviction that there is only one way to teach it as every student, teacher, lecturer or adviser has a different way of stimulating movement in children and others.

Dance should provide the opportunity to experience creative and expressive movement; the opportunity for movement memory training, and also the experience of dancing alone, with a partner and in small and large groups. Vocal, percussive, musical, or vocal and musical accompaniment can be dealt with as a separate task, but must be brought in whenever possible throughout all stages of the work. The accompaniment can either be imposed on the dancers, or made by the dancers themselves.

The factor to be considered when teaching dance is the amount of suggestion for ideas and material that needs to be given. This depends upon the needs and experience of a class—above all the teacher must take what she can from the children and help them to use their ideas and develop them. Help can be given in many ways—by setting the dramatic situation (a skeleton framework), by giving suggestions for dramatic ideas, by the use of expressive sounds, words and rhythms, by the use of sound alone, or by the use of movement alone. Children need to be made aware of the use of big, bold movements and shadow or echo movements, of effort movements and their derivatives and of the use and application of these in a dance situation.

Many people confuse basic movement and the art of movement. The art of movement is the work of the Art of Movement Studio where basic movement as such is a training period for students and is not to be taught to children as training exercises. The educational programme consists of Laban's sixteen movement themes. Basic movement is the product of physical educationalists applying Laban's principles to physical education techniques and producing a movement education of their own—the West Riding of Yorkshire being one of the foremost authorities in this work.

Everyone must, of course, decide for themselves which school of thought to pursue. In the author's opinion it would seem that neither on its own is sufficient. Some of Laban's movement themes as such do not produce the educational effect or pure mastery of movement and technical skill in performance as required by some people, while basic movement or movement education *per se* without the use of apparatus, dance or dance-drama situations can become boring to children over a long and extended period.

As the children need both skill (a movement vocabulary or a science of movement) and in addition an art of movement (expressive and aesthetic as well as creative), it would seem that basic movement and basic movement into dance leading directly into dance composition, dance mime and dance drama could well be the solution to the problem in dance teaching as well as in other branches of physical education.

Regardless, however, of different opinions and views, physical educationalists have now acknowledged a profound debt to Laban's work, which came into education largely through the efforts of the physical educationalists. Is it not time that the two—the art of movement and basic movement or physical education in its various forms were definitely welded together into a form of movement education? The result could well mean less argument, less confusion amongst teachers and better movement opportunities for children. The stage where children have acted as guinea-pigs for different ideas in movement—whatever it be called—should now be past. It should be possible for the art of movement and physical education to merge without the complete annihilation of one by the other. The emphasis is surely on merger between the two, not the complete submergence of one by the other; it should not be a question of which is the main and dominant branch, and which the subsidiary.

All branches of physical education have a common root factor—that is, they are all concerned with movement of children, by children and for children, and it is possible for all branches to have a common aim whilst developing in their own way and making their own particular contribution to a movement programme without losing their individuality. This surely is the aim and the test of assessing the worth of any educational process in any subject of the school curriculum —namely, that it is part of a whole educational programme, nothing of which can be viewed as an entirety in itself, or exist in a vacuum by itself.

The important factor in school life is the total and complete education of a child, not a child educated in many different subjects and in many isolated parts. The particular label given to any branch of movement education, the particular way of teaching it, the philosophy or concept propounded, the arguments for or against are all of little value if it has no relevance to child education or makes no appeal to children. Anyone who has taught children for a great number of years will know that the success or failure of any movement idea or process of physical education to be adopted as a "prospective candidate" rests upon the ability of the teacher to teach it, and even more important, upon the reception of the idea by the child and his ability to make use of it. Children themselves are expert in assessing what has or has not value, what will or will not work, what is or is not suitable for their needs. In any process of education they expect that they themselves should be the first consideration, and object to being used for the sole purpose of proving that one method of teaching, or one branch of physical education, or one teacher, is better than another.

Most demonstration classes in any method or in any branch of movement are carefully rehearsed with chosen children in order that they successfully demonstrate that which they are required to show. One always shows perfection in order to qualify, evaluate and justify methods of physical education—why does one not, in addition, show completely unrehearsed classes so that the spectators may watch the processes of introduction, reception by the children and growth, and may more clearly and fairly judge if these be present?

It could be said that many educationalists, whatever their particular role, are seeking entertainment, self-fulfilment and self-justification rather than education. One must not assume that there is only one way of educating children, whatever the particular branch of education; neither should one assume that every child needs the same method, or that one method is suitable for everybody; especially since the method often changes after introduction and before it has had a chance to be consolidated and truly examined. It is unwise to assume that every teacher is capable of teaching expertly the current method in vogue whether it evokes a response in her as a teacher or not.

The great value of Laban's work is that it is consistent in its aims and values and has, at the same time, sympathetic consideration for other ideas. Laban's work fits in with the rest of the world and does not require the rest of the world to adjust to Laban's work. If the work is developed or expanded, it is done for a valid purpose, not merely to provide a means by which teachers may achieve bigger and better jobs and salaries, which further remove them from actual teaching and contact with children. Laban's work is content to be its own justification; it rests upon the acquisition of one's own personal technique and does not rely upon a teacher who is skilful and clever at imposing her technique upon children, and at using children in order to demonstrate the foolproof quality of her ideas and work.

In teaching educational or creative dance in simple terms there are certain aims—the teaching of dance composition, dance mime and dance drama. Dance mime and dance drama should give experience of body and facial movement, dramatic qualities and inner attitudes—the expression of personality. Dance composition should give experience of body movement, different rhythms, shapes and phrasing, step patterns and the experience of building up movement motifs. In addition we have the teaching of the motion factors, occupational rhythms, and dimensional scale activities.

DANCE COMPOSITION

Step patterns in meeting and parting. "Swedish Rhapsody" by Alfrén is the suggested music for this composition. The children should create a step using different parts of the feet, for example, a heel and toe step, which fits in with the rhythm of the music. Part of the step should be on the spot and part travelling away. The step should be executed in all directions using both legs and both sides of the body. The children travel towards a partner and the step is then executed first to the right and then to the left, travelling sideways, facing a partner. In the third part they join with partner and dance together on the spot, about the spot and about the room using a common step arrived at by mutual consent. The children then separate, moving away from partners to resume the first part of the dance, that is, their own personal step freely moving about.

Progress in this case starts with the experience of dancing alone, leads to meeting a partner and dancing with them, then finishes with parting to dance alone again, using step patterns and different aspects of space to do this.

Group Reaction. "Echo Four Two" by Laurie Johnson is the suggested music for this dance composition. The main theme is group reaction. The class should make groups of four with one group acting as the centre or focus. This is the first group to start moving—faintly at first, with shadow movements (faint movements echoing the main force movements) building up in strength until they are working at maximum effort force. The other groups maintain absolute stillness. The central group then split and dance off to the other groups, waking them up and initiating the movement of other groups by their own. As before, the movement starts faintly at first building up to maximum strength. All groups then split and everyone dances as an individual until the main or central group take the initiative again by driving all back to their original groups in the original starting positions where the movement fades and they resume absolute stillness in stationary positions. The central group then dance back to their original group starting position where the dance fades completely.

Meeting and parting using efforts. "Tonight" from the musical *West Side Story* is the suggested music for this composition. Individual dancers start on the low level with rising and falling or lifting and sinking movements gradually leading up to full extension and into turning on the spot. This leads into the class forming groups of three in a held position of freeze or stillness. In the groups a motif is established of swaying and balancing to the music incorporating turns away from and towards the group focal point. The dancers then break away completely from the group formation with running, leaping, turning into held positions. Using this sequence they meet a partner and together establish a motif or sequence of swaying on the spot and travelling about the room together. Resumption of the original groups of three then follows to build up a group improvisation. The dance ends with all three dancers in sequence leaping out of the group into a position of strength, and when this is done all turn to finish on the low level. Meeting and parting with effort is the main theme here.

Jazz ballet. Jazz ballet to the record *Our Favourite Melodies* (Elgin, Rogers and Farrell). This consists of the following:

(*a*) Gestures—with various parts of the body, in different directions on various levels—facial gestures also can be included. A gesture can be done travelling or on the spot.

(*b*) Leaps—with arms and legs in various positions making various shapes using different directions. Leaps are used for travelling or locomotion purposes.

(*c*) Pose or held positions—with body in various shapes using various levels and directions. These are on the spot positions.

(*d*) Steps—an innumerable variety can be used and can be executed travelling or on the spot.

It is important to stress that body movement is an essential factor with the above. A sequence is made up using (*a*)–(*d*) in any order, but one must lead into another in order to make the sequence continuous and the pose or held positions must be maintained to stress the use of arrested flow. The main content here is going and stopping.

Stepping, leaping and stretching. "Valse Coppélia" from the ballet *Coppélia* by Delibes is the suggested music for this composition. The class start by finding various ways of leaping into space and stretching on the spot where they land. They then build up and establish a sequence consisting of a step pattern which moves to the right side, to the left side, leading into a leap forward into a stretch position on the spot and repeat, etc. A second sequence is then built up of successive leaps ending in a stretch position with running, turning and twisting movements interposed between each sequence of leaping and stretching. The dancers then revert to the first sequence established and the composition ends with individual creative movement to the music. This can be further developed into partner or group work if desired.

DANCE MIME

It is here important to differentiate between dance mime and dance drama. Dance mime is the sole use of face and body, whilst in dance drama use is made in addition of the sung or spoken word.

Bailiffs. Work with a partner—one partner establishes the character of a big, tough, fat bailiff, and the other the character of a householder, for example:

(*a*) a downtrodden weepy little woman, or

(*b*) a scolding shrew, or

(*c*) a fussy evasive little woman, or

(*d*) a big fat woman with a rolling pin who calls to her husband for aid or who sets the dog on to the bailiff.

Build up the dramatic situation by the bailiff knocking on the door and demanding the rent. There is no reply so he knocks again more insistently this time. The householder answers and a dramatic interplay is built up between the two of you according to your individual character portrayals. The result or resolution of the situation is again according to your character, for example:

(*a*) Does the bailiff get the rent?

(*b*) Does he go away beating a hasty retreat?

(*c*) Is he chased off by the dog?

(*d*) Does he finish up sympathising with the poor weepy little woman who cannot pay the rent?

The children should change over so that they have a turn at being both characters—the bailiff and the householder.

House on fire! Imagine your house is on fire. What do you do? Do you:

(*a*) prance around in anguish going frantic with grief but utterly helpless and unable to do anything about it?

(*b*) run for help and plead with other people to help you?

(*c*) ring up the fire brigade?

No one will believe that your house is on fire or help you. Again what do you do? Do you:

(*a*) plead more desperately for help?

(*b*) bang down the telephone in a rage?

(*c*) try to put the fire out yourself?

What is the eventual result? Do you:

(*a*) get help at long last?

(*b*) succeed in putting the fire out yourself?

(*c*) watch it burn sobbing with anguish, or think with glee of insurance money, or adopt an attitude of fortitude and resignation?

Thus by building up a question and answer situation the teacher can stimulate the class to expressive movement of face and body depicting various dramatic situations.

A letter! Imagine that you wake up in the morning, you hear the postman arrive, get up, go downstairs and you see the letter! Show by your body and face whether you are expecting or dreading this letter. Pick it up according to your expectations, for example, do you seize upon it eagerly or reluctantly and slowly reach out for it? Open it, again depicting by facial and bodily expression whether you are reluctant or in eager haste to do so. How do you read this letter—slowly or quickly? Show by your facial expression what the contents are, for example, it is good news—you have won a lot of money, been left a legacy, etc.—or is it bad news—the death of a relative, or a blackmail note, or a bill you cannot pay? Again show by your face and body how you react to the situation, for example, do you dance with glee, faint, or weep bitterly, etc.?

Thus by suggestive questions the teacher can stimulate the class to build up a situation of action and reaction depicted with bodily and facial expression.

Dreams. Show by your face and body that you are asleep. You have a dream—what kind is it? Is it a pleasant one, a nightmare of horror or an exciting one? Show by your face and body which kind of dream you are experiencing. You wake up—again show how you wake according to the nature of your dream, for example, do you wake sobbing with fright, or fighting mad, or cheering madly? Now show what you do when you are fully awake, for example, do you light a cigarette shaking still, or mop up the tears and get back into bed, or telephone a friend or the police, or shoot yourself, etc.?

Here again the dramatic situation is built up by one action leading to or stimulating another according to mood, feeling or the actual situation chosen by the children.

Wanted! Imagine you are a fugitive on the run—what do you do? Do you run madly here and there in a panic, or slink from one doorway to another, or mingle with a crowd trying to lose yourself in it, or attempt to disguise yourself, for example, by pulling your hat down over your eyes, etc.? Are you being followed? If so show what you do about this situation, for example, do you kill the person who is following you, or yourself, or do you get away, etc.?

In prison. Imagine you are in prison. Show by your face and body how you react to this situation, for example, are you in despair, in a rage and fury, or in an apathetic stupor, etc.? A fire now breaks out in the prison—what is your reaction? Do you try to get help, do you frantically try to escape, or do you shake the prison bars in an anguish of fear, etc.? You manage to get out—what is your reaction to the strange, almost forgotten world outside? Now imagine you are seeking your friends or relatives. Show by your face and body what is the nature and result of your search.

Fighting a partner. Choose a weapon with which to fight; it can be the same as your partner's or a different one. Show by your movement which weapon you have chosen, for example, sword, pistol, fists, etc., and prepare for the fight—practise a few slashes with a sword, or prime and take aim with your pistol. Now develop the actual fight situation with your partner and show what is the result of this fight—are you wounded, killed, or do you run away, etc.? If you are the victor, show what are your reactions after the fight when it is all over—are you filled with remorse or exultation at your victory? How do you dispose of the body?

Urchins. Be an urchin—move about establishing this character using body and face to do so, for example, by making rude gestures, kicking stones about in the gutter, etc. Practise urchin actions, for example, throwing stones. Now establish a movement motif for an urchin, for example, bound and bound and bound about and then on the spot stop and look about, or bound and bound and bound about and then on the spot stop and make a rude gesture, or saunter and saunter and saunter about and then on the spot stop and make a rude gesture. Thus try to establish a step pattern with this movement motif which will combine with dramatic gestures on the spot. This can then be taken a stage further by building up another movement motif which indicates by bodily and facial gesture that you are robbing a pie shop and a dramatic situation is then built up by showing how you rob the shop, what happens as a result of this and what is the conclusion to this episode.

At the races. Imagine you are at a race-course and with your *back* to me show me what is happening to your horse, for example, is it winning, has it fallen at the first fence, or is it last in the race, etc.? Show how you are reacting to the chosen situation. Now show what happens after the race, for example, have you won, are you robbed of your winnings by a pick-pocket, what happens if you have lost heavily— do you shoot yourself or try to borrow more money to back again, etc.?

After the first dramatic establishment the class may then turn round and have unlimited use of the space.

Old ladies and young urchins. Work with a partner and establish contrasts in movement with the character and movement motif of a fussy, twittering, light old lady with affected mannerisms in contrast or as against the strong, bold movements of an uncouth urchin who is making fun of her. Establish characters and movement motifs for both of these personalities and change round so that you have a turn at both establishing facial gestures as well. Now select one character and build up the dramatic situation between self and partner, for example, the old lady enters followed by the urchin who is making fun of her. She scolds him and lunges at him with her umbrella, etc. The situation is resolved by the intervention of the appearance of a policeman, for example, the urchin runs off and the old lady continues on her way.

On the park bench! Two characters should be established, one of a boy and one of a girl. Start by both sitting on the bench depicting their attitudes, for example, a shy girl with a boy who wishes to make advances to her. Show how the boy does this and what is the girl's reaction—does she slap his face, kick him off the bench or run away, etc.? What is the eventual result—does the boy end up proposing to the girl, or do they fall out, etc.? This can be done, as an alternative, with a bold, forward girl making advances to a shy boy.

Again give the children the experience of being both characters by changing round. Later a definite choice for one or the other can be made if desired.

Animal motifs. The movement should portray the particular movements and gestures of the animal chosen, for example, a cat. Here the movement can be indicative of the cat curling up asleep followed by waking up and stretching as cats do. This can be followed by the cat washing itself, scratching itself, sharpening its claws, etc. The sequence can also include a cat "mouse-watching" or arching its back, spitting and fluffing out its tail upon encountering a dog, etc.

Behind the door. The mood should be mysterious and hesitancy and fear should be expressed by the body and in the face. Imagine that you see before you a door which is dark and forbidding—show what your first reactions are. Go up to the door, knock on it and then listen intently. Repeat this sequence. Then try the door, push it open and go through. Show that you are now moving along a dark corridor, listening for sounds and feeling your way in the darkness. As you move down this corridor it gets brighter—show that you can proceed more confidently than before. At the end of the corridor there is a brilliantly lit room—show what you find there, for example, is it something horrible or wonderful? What are your reactions, for example, do you faint, etc.? Hold your last position for a finishing movement to the sequence.

DANCE DRAMA

The bull-fight. This is both single and partner work—one person being the bull and the other the matador. The sequence starts with both moving freely about the room according to the character. The matador then makes a grand entrance into the ring—acknowledges the crowd, etc. Make up a motif to do this. The bull then enters—here again make up a motif for the bull. The matador must show his reaction to the bull and a subsequent interplay must be built up between bull and matador to show the actual fight itself. How does the fight end?

Make up your own motifs, for example, a bull motif could be to paw and paw and paw the ground and then charge! A matador motif could be to swirl and swirl and swirl his cape and with an "*Olé*" swirl and pirouette right round, etc. Various sounds can be used with the movements of bull and matador, for example, "*¡Olé!*," "*¡toro!*," etc., and snorting sounds.

Fireworks. Show by your movement what kind of firework you are, for example, rocket, squib, golden rain, wheel, bomb, etc. Make up a firework motif with the appropriate sound accompaniment. This then leads to group activity, arranging the groups to start in the shapes of the various fireworks chosen. One group, perhaps the squibs, can start moving and thus initiate the movement of the other groups as they are set alight. Thus we get a movement reaction of one group to another. An alternative is to start with all the fireworks in one big group on the bonfire and build up the movement reaction of which group starts first and passes on or sets off the other fireworks with all going off at different times. Thus we should get a cacophony of movement and sound. The sequence ends with the fireworks burning up and dying out with all ending in a spent and burnt out finishing position. The starting and finishing positions are just as important as the movement sequence itself.

Witches. Show that you are a witch, for example, have a deformed body shape, cackle with laughter with a funny face and sharp, bony, spiky hands. Move about in this character and establish a motif. Now make a spell to destroy your enemy—collect ingredients, for example, rat, frog, lizard's gizzard, etc., to put into your cauldron. Make it quite clear in bodily and facial movement what you are putting into the cauldron—descriptive sounds and words for each ingredient may be used. Stir your cauldron and incite the flames to rise and dance round. Here again make use of magic words and sounds to assist the movement. This can be done singly or in groups. Now build up the dramatic sequence and mood by peering anxiously into the cauldron to see if your spell has worked. The climax is to show the result of the spell, for example, do you see your enemy dying in the flames and rub your hands in glee? Or has the spell not worked and in a screaming rage do you destroy all your equipment by kicking the cauldron over, etc.? Or again does the spell react on you personally—do you die writhing in agony?

It is important in all dramatic work to give the children a chance to move about freely at first in character in order to become fully absorbed and enclosed in the mood of same before moving on to a more directed and storytelling sequence. Again, the finishing and starting positions are important— children can never really become absorbed and establish any progressive sequence if allowed to start and finish without due concentration.

A witches' sabbath and a witch hunt. Come to the witches' sabbath secretively and cautiously, perhaps riding in on a broomstick. Huddle into groups and discuss witch matters until a hush falls over all for Satan is arriving. Move into a space on your own showing fear and apprehension of the master. In your space establish a motif of paying homage to the devil, for example, bow and scrape with cries of "Homage, Master", etc. Ask, pray and beseech him to give you evil powers. Build this motif up to a climax of *absolute stillness*! Go into a trance after this dramatic pause, show in movement that you are possessed and rejoice in your evil power. Again build up to a climax of absolute stillness after all this frenzied movement.

Suddenly there is the sound of a drum beat which signifies that soldiers and people are approaching—the witch hunt is on! Show how you panic! What can you do? Do you work a spell—put a cloud between you and them or try to "dart them dead" using eyes and hands? Or do you run and the chase is on, or stand and curse and scream at them? They catch you and drag you to the stake and burn you. Show your reaction to the flames, for example, writhe in agony shrieking abuse, burn to a cinder and die, or turn into a vulture and escape. Again establish a finishing position or exit flight to finish the sequence.

The Pied Piper. Various characters from this story, related by Robert Browning in his poem *The Pied Piper of Hamelin,* can be chosen to portray in dramatic movement, for example:

- (*a*) the Pied Piper,
- (*b*) children including the lame boy,
- (*c*) Lord Mayor and Council Members,
- (*d*) village people—men and women,
- (*e*) rats.

Having experimented and then selected your particular character, establish a motif for same. As this is a large group dance drama a dramatic build up or establishment is essential in the following suggested stages.

STAGE 1 Enter the villagers complaining about the rats—a ferment of protest and action in movement. They band together and in a procession head to the mayoral chambers to an established rhythm and step, for example, stamp—stamp—stamp, with fists shaking to the cry of "Rats—Rats—Rats." All go out doing this.

STAGE 2 Entrance of rats with rat activity, for example, eating cheese, falling into vats, etc., to descriptive sound of the actual poem. Vocal sound is here made use of to stimulate and keep alive the movement. All rats then make a scurrying exit.

STAGE 3 Enter the children playing and shouting with the lame boy hobbling along.

STAGE 4 Enter the Pied Piper with an established dance motif. Build up the reaction of the children to this strange man. The Piper dances alone for a while then the children join in and all go out.

STAGE 5 Enter the Mayor and Council who gather round discussing the problem of rats. Here one can build up an interplay of movement efforts, for example, the Mayor *presses* (pushes) to the Council—one member *shivers*—another *defies* him, etc. Enter villagers shouting and threatening—here again build up the dramatic interplay of the two opposing parties.

STAGE 6 There is a loud knock followed by silence! Enter the Piper with his established dance motif. All others freeze into group patterns. The Piper then makes his bargain with the Mayor and all go out, except the Piper who dances alone, until the rats begin to creep in slowly at first and then faster and faster until all are in a merry dance which ends with the Piper leading the rats off to destruction.

STAGE 7 Enter the Mayor, Council and villagers all rejoicing. Show great jubilation and follow the poem in the actual activity which took place, for example, ringing of bells, etc. Enter the Piper again who demands his money—the Mayor refuses and he goes out with all after him booing and laughing at his discomfiture.

STAGE 8 Re-enter Piper alone again with his own dance motif. As he plays the children come in, as the rats did and the same merry dance ensues leading to exit with the lame boy hobbling after the others.

STAGE 9 Enter Mayor, Council and village people frantic with fear and anxiety searching for the children and calling for them to come back. Build up the dramatic interplay between the two opposing parties again which ends with the Mayor sending out his plea and proclamation.

STAGE 10 Enter the lame boy and a realisation of doom should come over all which deepens as he relates his story in movement and/or words. All end in finishing positions showing utter dejection, despair and misery.

It should be observed that the dance drama work in this chapter has been gradually built up from single to partner to small group to large group work. This is essential, for it is unwise to expect children to cope with a full scale story from the onset. It is obvious that one story may not be completed in one lesson and thus it is always necessary to recapitulate a little each time to capture the full mood and to progress, and this requires experience. Also it will be obvious that in full-scale stories certain solo parts are necessary which require the more experienced and gifted dramatic dancers who are not immediately obvious when starting dance mime and drama.

The build-up for this particular dramatic dance has been purposely stressed and meticulously outlined for the benefit of the teacher. With experienced staff and children it is possible to proceed at a faster and less deliberate pace and to enlarge and embellish to a much greater degree as will be illustrated below. Whether music, the particular poem or both are used for the *Pied Piper* is entirely a matter of choice depending upon the needs, abilities and experience of a particular class, as is the question as to whether the teacher or the pupils act as narrator or speak the words if the poem itself be used. With more experienced children it is advantageous to combine this movement experience with that of creative writing and to allow the children to add their own verbal contribution or indeed write their own story if desired.

Exodus from Egypt (music—"Theme from Exodus" by E. Gold).

STAGE 1—*Depiction of slavery*. All start in a position depicting slavery and dejection either singly or in groups. In movement, depict the shrinking away from this life, the horrors of endurance, the maimed bodies, the lack of hope, etc. Facial expression is important as well as bodily expression. Lead from this into a working motif depicting the agonies this produces—the writhing away from the lash, the feebleness of body effort, the defiance, hope or apathy of mood. This in turn leads to the hour or time of rest when physical effort is over for the moment. Out of this rest period must come the resurgence of hope arising and then dying, the gathering together of a few strong ones left for rebellion and escape.

STAGE 2—*The emergence of Moses*. A single strong character emerges from the group who bands the people together with the assenters and dissenters, puts new hope and vitality into the weak and leads them all out of the land of slavery.

STAGE 3—*The Exodus* (music—the H.M.V. Living Classics record (A.L.P. 1936) "Let My People Go," from the series "The Living Bible"; read by Sir Laurence Oliver). Dramatic movement illustrating this by vocal sound, stimulated by and arising from this sound. On the main theme words "Let my people go"—a general united pleading movement upwards from the whole group should be estabilished, followed by a sinking in despair at the refusal. When release is finally granted the climax to this dance drama can be reached either by a general group movement of a sigh of release which ends in a finishing position or by a movement which rises and falls until it reaches and lifts up all the group to a moving exit.

If a further conflict is desirable characters of soldiers and the character of Pharaoh himself can be introduced, but in the initial stages children can cope with only one character at a time; the inclusion of others can be a suitable progression or can be included immediately, if desired, with experienced or exceptionally gifted classes. This particular dance drama is highly suitable for seniors experienced or otherwise and with suitable adaptation can be used for top juniors.

Lepers—"The Lepers' Search for the Christ" from the record *Musical Highlights* (music *from Ben-Hur* (Miklos Rozsa)).

The first essential is to show the bodily and facial results of leprosy as the lepers come creeping out of their holes and hiding places. The loneliness and isolation must be built up by showing their lack of contact with other people, for example, the sight of relatives who come with food but stand afar off, or the way in which they themselves creep down to the outskirts of a village, ringing their bells, to gaze on the life from which they are debarred. The next phase is the coming of Christ and their plea for healing, the realisation of his powers and the miracle that happens when their bodies are made whole and strong again. The climax is the thanksgiving and the way in which each individual reacts to his cure.

This again is more suitable for senior pupils. Great care should be taken by the teacher in choosing descriptive words and sentences in order to describe the situation and thus stimulate the ideas and movement of the pupils. In the author's opinion it is generally unwise to have children portraying Christ as many find this very difficult, as they do in a dance drama dealing with the Creation of the World, which is a popular favourite, and in which one child may dance the Spirit of God. It often leads to self-consciousness, or on the other hand, over-confidence or to emotional upsets, and until one is absolutely sure that a particular child can handle the matter with confidence and in true dance perspective, a lighting arrangement such as a spot light can be equally if not more effective and does not so easily distract the attention and occupation of other children.

The death camp (music—"Legend of the Glass Mountain" (Nino Rota) and "Song of the Mountains" (Ortelli-Pigarelli).

To the slow beat of a drum come out of the camp, after release, in slow procession. Drop by the wayside to sleep and dream reliving the horrors of the past. Here the music is used to stimulate movement and express the experiences. Go further back into the past before these events occurred; this is a softer dream than the nightmare that preceded it. The climax is the awakening and the resumption of life.

This again is more suitable for senior pupils than any other age group. It should be noted, however, that a basic idea emerges which is applicable to all age groups and their particular ideas and work. This is that after a lengthy dance drama it is advisable to perform a short one in order to retain absorption and contact without tiring and satiating the creative and expressive qualities of the children. Furthermore, as the children become more experienced they should tackle more demanding ideas and, or as an alternative, a mere skeletal framework, as illustrated in the "Death Camp" dance drama, should be given in order that the ideas in bodily and facial movement and expression are solely those of the children.

THE MOTION FACTORS

These are Space, Weight, Time and Flow, or, in other words, where we go, how we go and for how long we go.

1. *Space.* This is the discovery, awareness and use of space around the body whilst on the spot, whilst moving about the spot or about the room. It also includes the difference between different body shapes, that is, stretched, bent (curled) and twisted. The pathway that one makes whilst using space can

be either straight or curved, *i.e.* direct or indirect. It also includes the use of space by oneself or in small or large groups.

2. *Weight.* This is the discovery, awareness and use of the amount of force (*i.e.* strong and light) put into movements which can be done by using the whole or part or parts of the body.

3. *Time.* This is the discovery, awareness and use of the speed (*i.e.* quick or slow) put into movements which can be done by using the whole or part or parts of the body.

4. *Flow.* This is the discovery, awareness and use of the duration of movements. Movements may continue without pause or may come to a sudden stop.

The principles to be considered are the four motion factors mentioned above, the six movement elements—strong, light, quick, slow, direct and indirect—incorporated within them and the eight basic efforts or actions and their derivatives which are classified by Rudolf Laban as illustrated by the following table.

Basic efforts and their derivatives

Basic effort	Derivative
Pressing	Crushing, Cutting, Squeezing
Flicking	Flipping, Flapping, Jerking
Punching or Thrusting	Probing, Piercing, Shoving
Floating or Flying	Strewing, Storing, Stroking
Wringing	Stretching, Pulling, Plucking
Dabbing	Pulling, Tapping, Shaking
Slashing	Beating, Throwing, Whipping
Gliding	Smoothing, Smearing, Smudging

The classification of basic efforts according to the six movement elements are as follows:

Pressing is strong, direct, sustained.
Flicking is light, indirect, quick.
Thrusting is strong, direct, quick.
Floating is light, indirect, sustained.
Wringing is strong, indirect, sustained.
Dabbing is light, indirect, quick.
Slashing is strong, indirect, quick.
Gliding is light, direct, sustained.

Every bodily action or derivative contains a certain three of the six movement elements. By expressing these various actions or efforts in a variety of ways and in sequences, the child experiences movement over a wide field and thus opportunity is given for *purposeful* creative movement. After the child has been given this initial experience as part of the basic movement or dance lesson, it needs then to be made aware of how to use this experience in various dance situations as illustrated below.

THE TEACHING OF EFFORTS THROUGH DANCE DRAMA AND MIME

Red Riding Hood and the Wolf. Characters can be chosen and established:

(*a*) Red Riding Hood,
(*b*) Wolf,
(*c*) Grandmother,
(*d*) Woodcutter.

Establish a movement motif by making up an effort sequence to portray the character chosen, with a dramatic basis. Examples are as follows:

(*i*) Red Riding Hood picks flowers on the way to her grandmother by dabbing movements from side to side, turns round on the spot and sniffs her flowers, *e.g,* dab-dab-dab-float and sniff.

(*ii*) The Wolf coming through the woods bounds and bounds and bounds and sniffs the ground and in the air.

(*iii*) The Grandmother in her cottage wheezes and wheezes and coughs and staggers into bed.

(*iv*) The Woodcutter swings and swings and swings his axe and then chops off the Wolf's head.

These examples can then be built up by groups of the four characters into a story where Red Riding Hood dances through the forest and meets the Wolf, with dramatic interplay. She waves goodbye, blows him a kiss and continues on her way. The Wolf then visits Grandmother with the subsequent dramatic interplay for the story. Red Riding Hood visits the Wolf who is posing as Grandmother until the entrance of the Woodcutter and the end of the story. Sound used to stimulate appropriate effort movements or sequences can be brought in here; for example, Red Riding Hood's remark "What big teeth you have Grandma" can stimulate pressing movements from Red Riding Hood as she leans forward to examine her grandmother, and chopping movements from the Wolf as he snaps at her.

Creatures from outer space. Be a Martian or a creature from outer space—move about with an unearthly body and face making appropriate movements and noises. Form groups and make up a dominating effort sequence to dominate and take over the planet Earth. A group noise as well as a group movement should arise from this. The strongest and most dominating group movement takes over the other, or weaker groups, until we have one total big group movement. This should then proceed to a programme for invasion with its chosen and subsequent results as to whether the invaders take over or perish in their attempt. This can progress to two opposing forces, invaders from outer space and defenders from Earth battling it out, and the use of space ships, robots, ray-guns, etc., can also be brought in if desired.

A village scene. Efforts are again used for movement motifs for different characters as follows:

(*a*) The Mayor who presses from one side to the other, and then down in the middle with his seat.

(*b*) The Gossips who flicker and flutter and chatter in groups saying "Gossip, gossip, gossip" in a light flickering voice as they do so.

(*c*) The Scamps who bound and cartwheel and somersault, and punch and fight and throw stones.

This can be built up in a dramatic interplay sequence where everyone comes in and moves about in their own movement motif, collecting and banding together in character groups to establish a group movement. With dramatic interludes and interplay between groups the story can then follow any chosen direction and end.

Passage from Shakespeare's Richard III, Act V, Scene 3—"Despair and Die." Find different ways of saying this particular passage where the ghosts come to Richard in his nightmare on the eve of the big battle. This will produce different efforts for different dramatic movements for different characters. Anne, his wife, is, for example, an ethereal, light, waving character in movement and sound effort, whilst the man drowned in the barrel of wine is thunderous and threatening.

Goldilocks and the Three Bears. Again establish effort sequences according to chosen character as follows:

(*a*) Father Bear who is pressing and fierce. He presses from side to side, from down to up and growls. Establish a rhythm for this movement motif, for example, press and press and press and pre...ss and growl loudly.

(*b*) Mother Bear who is bustling and energetic and who bustles about quickly several times and then on the spot exhales long and slowly in a deep sigh.

(*c*) Baby Bear who is angry and peevish who slashes and stamps when he discovers Goldilocks has used his personal possessions and finally howls with rage when he finds her in his bed. Establish a rhythm, for example, stamp and stamp, shake your paw in rage, break down and sob and howl loudly and strongly. Throw yourself to the floor kicking with temper, fists flying with rage.

(*d*) Goldilocks who is light with happy, gay, floating and dabbing movements. Again establish a rhythm to match the effort sequence chosen, for example, a *pas de bas* step from one side to the other, turning right round and yawning delicately on the spot. When she is examining the food, the chairs and the beds an excellent opportunity arises for the use of efforts.

THE TEACHING OF OCCUPATIONAL RHYTHMS THROUGH DANCE DRAMA AND MIME

Occupational rhythms are the rhythm or time of movements used in various occupations, for example, the rhythm of digging or shovelling, or of housework. They can be taught in the same way as basic efforts, through dance drama and mime as illustrated below.

The Seven Dwarfs. Establish a character of a chosen dwarf in movement, facial expression and sound. The seven dwarfs are as follows:

- (*a*) Sneezy,
- (*b*) Sleepy,
- (*c*) Dopey,
- (*d*) Grumpy,
- (*e*) Happy,
- (*f*) Bashful,
- (*g*) Doc.

The next stage is to establish, in character, an occupational rhythm and action for the dwarfs, for example, digging with a spade or pick-axe, shovelling, clearing stones and rubble, hammering and chiselling, etc. This can be developed into a sequence of marching to work, actual working actions welded into a sequence and marching back home again. Each dwarf must maintain the dramatic movement, facial expression and sound (for example, Sneezy sneezes all the time, Sleepy yawns, etc.), throughout the whole sequence.

Good use can be made of the music from the film *Snow White and the Seven Dwarfs*, and this also includes the song "Whistle While You Work" which is ideal for occupational rhythms and actions dealing with Snow White's housework.

DIMENSIONAL SCALE ACTIVITY

Dimensional scale activity is, in its most simple and basic terms, the use of different directions and levels in space. Although it comes into all dance work, some people prefer to teach it as a theme or a lesson in itself. From the children's point of view, if this is to be done, it is preferable to approach it either by the invention of step patterns or by a dramatic approach rather than by a purely directed exercise or space harmony exercise. A simple dramatic sequence on the spot and travelling can have great appeal for children, for example, to reach up, plead and beg, leading to a sinking down in despair and grovelling on the ground or deep level. This can be followed by a reaching or running forward movement quickly leading in turn to a slow retreating or reaching movement or withdrawing backwards movement. A sideways movement going quickly and stopping suddenly from one side to the other can complete the sequence. Differences of time (speed) and weight (force) can thus also be brought in. Another idea is to fight with different weapons, for example, duelling with swords or pistols. Whatever the actual movements performed children require that movement should be related to experiences or ideas within their knowledge and ability; even senior pupils can find isolated movement themes too technical and boring for a movement or dance lesson where they expect the emphasis to be on moving as well as, or in relationship to, thinking. They can feel quite lost or frustrated at performing a routine or a series of movements, which, although different in concept and philosophy, in movement terms are not unlike the old Physical Training "drill."

GLOSSARY OF GYMNASTIC TERMS

Agility. An acrobatic movement requiring body mobility and ease.

Backward Squat. From a forward run, double take-off or jump transferring weight to hands turning immediately to land in backward sitting position; or the body passes over the apparatus backward and vertically with knees well drawn up to chest.

Cartwheel. A wheel-like movement where the body weight is transferred from hand to hand to foot to foot travelling sideways. Could be called a sideways handstand with legs apart.

Caterpillar Walk. In a tummy-towards-floor position, with weight on hands and feet, walk hands away from feet and then walk feet up to hands and continue thus.

Chinese Handstand. Bent leg crouch position, with weight on hands, with legs one on either side of the arms in front of the body, or with legs (knees) resting or propped on elbows one on either side at the back of the body.

Crab. Position of back bend or bridge, with weight on hands and feet, tummy-towards-ceiling position.

Crouch Jump. From a forward run or stationary position transfer weight from feet to hands in a bent body position with knees well drawn up to chest and seat high in the air.

Crouch Jump over Apparatus or Crouch Vault. From a forward run, double take-off, transferring weight to hands, going over (not round) the apparatus while travelling sideways in a bent-body position with knees well drawn up to chest.

Crow's Nest. From a reverse hanging position, on double ropes, arch the back to pull head upwards and backwards towards the feet so body swings in a cradle position with tummy facing the floor.

Double Take-off. Flight taking off from two feet.

Elbow Stand. Body in the vertical position with weight on hands, forearms and elbows with legs together stretched high in the air.

Extension Jump. Jump from single or double take-off with body in a stretched or extended shape.

Fence Vault. From a single take-off, the leg nearer the apparatus is swung up first and then joined by the other one. The body passes over the apparatus in a long sitting position leaning slightly back and legs lifted high. The weight is transferred from one hand to the other, the body landing sideways in line with the apparatus—one hand retaining contact with it.

Flip-Flap Movement. A dive or throwing movement where the body weight is thrown in a direction, *e.g.* forward, where the force of the leg swing and the curved or arched flight of the body, together with an additional push from hands if required, should bring the performer on to his/her feet.

Front Vault. From a single take-off the leg nearer the apparatus is swung forward with a hop, and then backward, and lifted backward and upward and joined by the other leg. The legs and body are in a straight line from the shoulders as the body passes over the apparatus in flight with weight on hands. The landing is sideways in line with the apparatus, one hand retaining contact with same.

Handspring. This could be called a "running handstand." From take-off into flight the body weight is transferred from hands to feet with a rapid "hands over heels" movement—the body turning over in the air passing through a position of handstand into flip-flap movement.

Handstand. Body in the vertical position with weight on hands (one or two) with legs stretched high in the air.

Headstand or Head and Hands Stand. Body in the vertical position with weight on hands and head (forehead) with legs stretched high in the air. In the author's opinion and in the terminology of children working in educational gymnastics this should be correctly termed a head *and* hands stand. A true headstand is where the weight is taken on the head solely.

Honey Pot in Threes. A means of lifting a performer where the middle or "lifted" person is in crouch position with knees fully bent, with legs crossed and hands on hips. The two supports at either side grasp his/her upper arms and swing him/her backwards and forwards and can then let go if desired.

Leap-frog. From a forward run, double take-off, transferring weight to hands to go over the apparatus with body in an upright position and legs astride.

Long Arm Swing. Swinging on or through apparatus with body weight on straight arms with body in an extended or stretched shape.

Longfly. From a forward run double take-off, transferring weight to hands to go over apparatus with body in a straight position and legs lifted backwards and above the apparatus in a split position. To continue off into a handspring, if desired, the legs are brought together and lifted so that the body is in a vertical position with weight on hands (handstand) with subsequent transference of weight on to feet on the floor with a flip-flap movement of the body to assist flight.

Monkey-Crawl. Moving along and underneath the bar with hands and crossed feet grasping same—feet moving first followed by hands and continue thus along.

Quick Squat. From a forward run, double take-off transferring weight on to hands over apparatus with body upright and head high. The knees should be up to chest and toes pointed.

Reverse Hanging. Position of stretch with body upside down on apparatus (handstand position almost) with weight on hands or hands and back of body according to which piece of apparatus is being used.

Roll. A "heels over head" movement in a curled position which can be performed forwards or backwards. From a squat-down position the body weight is tipped either forwards or backwards with transference of weight on to subsequent body parts, ending on feet. Legs may be stretched at the finish of the movement to make the roll lead into a forward or backward leg straddle or astride position if desired. This movement is usually referred to as a roll when performed along the floor or in contact with apparatus.

Screw Vault. From a forward run and double take-off the body is lifted with the weight well over the arms on the apparatus, with hips bent and knees bent under body in crouch position. The weight is then transferred to one arm and the body turns towards that arm and a twist is made in the air. This could be referred to as a vault with bent hips over apparatus and a reverse twist to land side towards the apparatus with one arm holding on to it, or it could equally be described as a "turning or twisting crouch jump."

Sheep Thro' the Gap. Keeping their arms straight the performer springs from a double take-off on to the apparatus (bar). The weight of the body then carries the performer backwards and forwards like a pendulum swinging from the hands. After several swings the performer arches the back to shoot the legs forward in a flip-flap movement to land on feet.

Shouldersault. From a forward run and double take-off the weight is taken on the apparatus on hands and back of neck and shoulder girdle with the head tucked well underneath. The legs are brought over the head in a stretched position apart and a flip-flap movement off the apparatus leads into flight into landing on feet.

Single Take-off. Flight taking off from one foot.

Slow Squat. From a forward run and double take-off, with weight on hands on the apparatus, the legs are brought up to chest and then straightened out in front of body to land. If as an alternative the legs are stretched out backwards first with a horizontal body position before the body passes through the arms, this can be termed "lift and squat" or "long arm back into front squat."

Somersault. This is a term which can be given to a roll when performed in the air or when the body is passing from the apparatus into flight.

Somersault Vault. From a forward run and double take-off, with weight on hands on the apparatus, the body performs a roll in the air to land on feet.

Standing Broad Jump. From a crouch squat position the arms are swung forwards and backwards like a pendulum. This leads to flight through the air with knees bent thrusting legs outwards and forwards to land.

Storming. From a forward run with a single take-off the body is propelled from the apparatus into the air in a stretched body position in flight before landing on feet. This could equally be termed an extension jump.

Thief. From a forward run with a single take-off from one leg the other leg is raised to lead forward. The take-off leg is then immediately raised to join the leading leg over the apparatus and weight is on hands to alight on feet.

Through Vault. From a forward run with a double take-off, with weight on hands, the knees are brought up to the chest and then straightened out by a strong thrust in flight to land on feet. This could be termed "long leg quick squat."

Trout-Up-Stream. A position of prone lying on front of body in a stretched horizontal position. The arms reach forward to pull the body along the apparatus while the head is lifted and the back arched and the total movement is then repeated.

Tuck Jump. The performer jumps from one or two feet with the body in a curled, crouch or squat position.

Upward Jump in Threes. Supporters stand sideways facing performer in the middle; with a shake hand grasp with one hand and elbow grasp with the other. The performer jumps in preparation and from a full knees bend is then lifted by the supporters into the air in an extension jump before landing again on feet.

Wolf. From a forward run with a double take-off the body is lifted over the apparatus on both arms and one leg is swung sideways. The weight is simultaneously transferred to the opposite arm as the leg is swung and the body passes vertically over the apparatus with one leg sent up to the chest and the other leg stretched sideways.

INDEX